Where's My Mustard?

How to Let Go, Attract and Achieve - A Quest to Self-Empowerment

Amy Lee Miller

Copyright © 2022 by **Amy Lee Miller**
Where's My Mustard?
How to Let Go, Attract and Achieve - A Quest to Self-Empowerment

All rights reserved. No part of this publication may be reproduced, distributed, or transmitted in any form or by any means, including photocopying, recording, or other electronic or mechanical methods, without the prior written permission of the publisher, except in the case of brief quotations embodied in critical reviews and certain other noncommercial uses permitted by copyright law.

Although the author and publisher have made every effort to ensure that the information in this book was correct at press time, the author and publisher do not assume and hereby disclaim any liability to any party for any loss, damage, or disruption caused by errors or omissions, whether such errors or omissions result from negligence, accident, or any other cause.

Neither the author nor the publisher assumes any responsibility or liability whatsoever on behalf of the consumer or reader of this material. Any perceived slight of any individual or organization is purely unintentional.

The resources in this book are provided for informational purposes only. Neither the author nor the publisher can be held responsible for the use of the information provided within this book.

ISBN: (hardcover) 979-8-9855768-4-9
ISBN: (paperback) 979-8-9855768-5-6
ISBN: (ebook) 979-8-9855768-3-2

Cover design by Alejandro Martin.
Printed in the U.S.A.

Thank you for purchasing *Where's My Mustard?* I'm excited to begin the journey with you. I'd also like to invite you to join my mailing list and stay connected for motivational content, offerings, and future books! As a thank you for opting in to my mailing list, I am extending an opportunity to connect with me for a complimentary one-on-one 30-minute coaching call if that is something that interests you. Subscribers will receive a link to my calendar to book your free session.

Subscribe today!

Here's to your success!
~Amy

https://coaching.beingamyleemiller.com

To all of my soul tribe members:

Thank you for everything I've learned from you so far. I'm excited to meet the rest of you.

TABLE OF CONTENTS

Introduction i
Chapter One: The Pull 1
    As You Overcome, You Become 3
Chapter Two: The Catalyst 19
    Your Deepest Pain Fuels Your Greatest Purpose 21
Chapter Three: The Quest 37
    Let Go, Allow, and Surrender 39
Chapter Four: Becoming a Mega-Manifester 55
    You Always Want More. How Do You Get It? 57
Chapter Five: Innocence Is Power 73
    Inexperience Allows the Element of Surprise 75
Chapter Six: The Answer Is in the Problem 103
    Change Your Perspective – Change Your Life 105
Chapter Seven: The Way to Win 119
    You Succeed at What You Focus On 121
Chapter Eight: Your Most Important Investment 137
    You Project How You Feel, Get Feeling Good 139
Chapter Nine: Vulnerability 159
    Your Greatest Strength Lies within Your Vulnerability 161
Chapter Ten: Beating Fear 173
    How to Never Make Another Mistake 175
Chapter Eleven: The Deep Stuff 189
    The Best Things Happen When You Have No Idea What's Next 191

Resources to Explore:	207
I Love Honesty	209
Acknowledgments	211
About the Author	213

Introduction

Do similar challenges keep showing up, leaving you feeling stuck in a certain area of your life? Perhaps you excel in your career but struggle to connect in meaningful relationships. Or maybe you're happy in your relationships but feel unfulfilled in your job.

Is there a nagging voice in the back of your mind whispering there's something bigger or different meant for you?

Are you constantly reminded of a stubborn curiosity that persists, despite your efforts to ignore it?

The challenges you face are not what determines your future. It's your actions, your choices, that lead you to where you end up. Have you considered your problems might be showing up for an important reason? What if once you overcome them, you become equipped to make your greatest impact, otherwise left unexplored? The fulfillment and connection you find when realizing your true place is waiting for you on the other side of your problems. Yet many of us choose to ignore the very catalyst set in place to get our attention.

While each of our challenges and goals will be different, the steps to overcoming and achieving are the same. When you learn how to pay attention to your emotions and better trust your instincts, you can navigate life with greater confidence and less resistance, becoming a magnet for your dreams that before seemed out of reach.

If you have something you want to accomplish and are searching for motivation, inspiration, and a newfound confidence that *yes, you can,* then this book is for you. If you're trying to let go of an uncomfortable emotion you've been carrying around, uncertain of where it's coming from and how to work through it, then read on.

Growing up unhappy and uncertain of why I couldn't shake the uncomfortable feeling I carried, I began my quest for self-improvement at a very young age. However, one thing I always had was the stringent belief in myself that I could achieve anything I set my mind to. For me, no goal has ever been too big, no challenge impossible to overcome. I allow myself the freedom to get and stay curious, trusting that whatever idea pops into my head is for a very good reason. I embrace each challenge with confidence, not knowing *how* I will surpass my next goal but knowing with unwavering certainty that I will. See it. Believe it. Achieve it.

But no matter how much I accomplished, my feeling of emptiness lingered. Whether I was by myself or with others, I felt alone and disconnected. I was determined to overcome this feeling of sadness. For the first half of my life, I awoke each morning to a feeling of dread. After learning and employing simple yet impactful practices over the years, I now wake each day with peace and with vigor, excited to get my day started. I'm now very happy almost all day, nearly every day. The purpose of this book is to help others get there faster. Whether your goal is to feel better or achieve more, it does not have to take decades or even years.

In this book, I share the concepts and mindset practices that allow me to achieve with more confidence and less effort. I share the tools and methods I learned to keep myself feeling good and

Introduction

attracting greater things. Along my path toward greater success and fulfillment, I also discovered perhaps the most profound awakening of all: the very cloud I so wanted to rid myself of, I was creating.

You are more powerful than you know. Through these pages, I will take you on the journey with me, the journey that led me to who I came to be, which is who I was always meant to be. You can change your life drastically by stepping out onto a new path that, while unfamiliar, you inherently know is calling you. Change can be scary. But sticking with what you know when you know you don't like it, in my opinion, is even scarier. Why let that be an option?

Since I was a very little girl, I knew I had a purpose, and living out this purpose, although I couldn't quite picture it just yet, remained my dominant focus. I have come to learn the things you want most in life often stay just out of reach until you do the deep inner work. Overcoming and becoming is just as painful as it is rewarding. But there is a reward on the other side.

From as far back as I can remember, maybe age six, and up until recent years, I felt uncomfortable. The place I felt most comfortable was when I was alone. Contradictory to how I felt on the inside, I was popular with the kids in school growing up. I always had a boyfriend of my choosing. It went like this:

On the first day of school, I would look around the classroom; I was on the hunt. I was also quite bossy, and some things don't change. I'd spot the boy I wanted to be my boyfriend, then tell him about it, and he would happily comply. If only life were that simple as you get older.

Despite my popularity and confidence in achieving what I set out to, on the inside, I was depressed. The strategies I learned and implemented helped me achieve goals while becoming a little happier and more fulfilled each year. Having such a strong belief in myself, I naturally have the same belief in others. My purpose became apparent—to help others believe in themselves with the same volition that I believe in myself. From a young age, I have always passionately encouraged others.

But to carry out my purpose on a greater scale, I first had to overcome some big emotional challenges myself. Your pain, I believe, is the catalyst that prepares you to show up as your best when the opportunity presents. Your opportunity will come, the chance to be and give your best, to make your most significant impact, but first, you have to build yourself up so that you have something to offer.

Life is hard. But would you believe me if I told you that it's only as hard as you make it on yourself? You do have choices, even when you're young. You can choose your thoughts, your attitude, whether or not to see your first step when it shows up and whether to be brave enough to take it. When you teach yourself that you can overcome a challenge, or achieve a goal, tackling obstacles the next time gets easier. What is familiar to you is easy, but there is always a first time. There is a first time to adopt a new mindset, push fear aside and step into who you are meant to be.

There have been many teachers along my path, some of whom may never know the significant impact they made. And through what I have learned, I've become strong and happy. I taught myself how to heal—anxiety, depression, and the false beliefs you tend to form about yourself when you're young that, until healed, can hold you back in your adult life. I've also taught myself how to achieve,

Introduction

be successful, and know *with certainty* that I will accomplish whatever I set my mind to.

My experiences, good and bad, my childhood (which was not the worst or the best by far), and my successes have all contributed to the contents of this book.

You are capable of uncovering your best self, feeling happy each day, letting go of your pain, making positive choices, and elevating your state of mind to a happy state most of every day.

In this book, I show you how you can feel better faster and adopt a winning mindset that instills greater self-confidence leading to success. I show you how to view your problems as tools instead of impossible obstacles and turn your frustration into momentum and focus.

I share the experiences that stimulated my seemingly endless quest to feel better, to keep overcoming so that I could ultimately *become*. I share the tough lessons I learned, key takeaways, and actionable steps I implemented to carry myself further; steps you can also take to propel yourself further and faster down your path toward success and greater happiness.

I share what I did to overcome the debilitating anxiety attacks that plagued me for more than twenty years. I share how, without medication, I beat my 30-plus-year struggle with depression. One thing about me is that I'm determined. Whatever I set my mind to, unless I learn along the way that it's not for me, I will achieve it. And so, that's what I have done, over and over throughout the twists and turns of my life. But my greatest achievement is that I'm happy.

The inherent belief I have in myself, that I can and will, is the same belief I have in others. The purpose of this book is to help you learn this about yourself. The things you desire are meant for you. And if there is a challenge in your way, that challenge is a catalyst to help you get the very thing you want, or perhaps you never knew you always wanted.

I believe the true definition of success is happiness. While others might admire your accomplishments, you likely won't feel successful if you're not happy doing what you do.

The things I've wanted most since I was very young are still what I desire most today—freedom, self-expression, and helping others through my self-expression. In addition to helping me overcome anxiety and depression, these drivers also led me to get into increasingly better shape, grow my income from each year to the next, become an entrepreneur, an author, a *Success and Leadership* coach, and to understand myself and those around me better. But most importantly, to feel happy and fulfilled.

Now I want to share the most important thing I've learned with you:

Yes, you can.

Can what? Whatever you wish.

And you can do it faster than you think. I'm sharing my secrets and vulnerability with you to help you get happier because a world of happy people is a better world.

As you read this book, I promise you will get to know yourself better. As a result, you will better understand those around you, creating an easier life and attracting better things.

Introduction

Your most important investment will always be yourself because the better you are and feel, the more you have to offer others. Why wait another minute to start being and feeling a little better today than you were yesterday?

I will probably make you laugh, and I will likely make you cry. In some parts, I may lose you, and that's okay; just push on and take in what resonates for now. I'll make you think. I will also tell you there's nothing in this book that you don't already know, at least somewhere deep down. Maybe it's just time for a reminder of the power you already have within you and that the answers you might be searching for could not be closer.

I'm cheering for you!
~*Amy*

Chapter One
The Pull

Chapter 1: The Pull

As You Overcome, You Become

"Turn your wounds into wisdom."
~*Oprah Winfrey*

Do you believe there is a deeper meaning in life, a greater purpose for your existence? Not sure? Here's an easier question. Do you ever *feel* like doing something?

If you could do anything and money were not an issue and failure were not possible, what would you do?

I like asking people this question and watching their eyes stop looking and instead begin wandering off to a place they perhaps haven't visited for a while. Curiosity is where creation starts.

If you've never ventured to ask yourself this question, *"If I could do anything, what would I do?"* then I challenge you to take a moment and ask yourself now. Second to your intuition, I believe curiosity can be your greatest strength when you employ it. If you could do anything, what would your *anything* look like? What would it feel like? If this question makes you uncomfortable, it's okay. The problem is not the question. The problem is your perspective, which you have the power to change. When you change your perspective, you change your life.

I have always believed that if a thought or an idea pops into your head, it's there for a reason. It's a clue. It's like when you're watching a movie, and you catch a moment early on that you somehow know is significant. It could be as innocent as a look or someone walking away. To the movie-watcher who's distracted, the moment seems like nothing. Yet when you're paying close attention, you know it's something.

I recently caught a moment like this when watching a drama movie about a team of CIA agents. The stakes were raised as they strategized their plan of action around a plane under siege by terrorists. The seemingly insignificant moment came in a lingering glance that I instinctively knew meant something. One character followed another character with his gaze as she got up to leave for a risky yet routine meeting. The significance of this short scene and the risky meeting that followed did not unfold until the end of the movie. Yet, while the moment had seemed like nothing, I later learned it was everything.

In the movies, they call this foreshadowing, a warning or indication of a future event. How much better are movies when you're paying attention? When you catch the little details, you feel like you're solving a mystery. You're curious and present. You're interested and invested. When you're engaged, you feel connected, following your observations as they later manifest into something bigger.

Real life is like the movies, or maybe, the other way around. Life gets better when you're paying attention. When you get an idea, seemingly out of nowhere, that manifests as curiosity; that idea has a purpose. And when you pay attention, you are easily led down the right path. You do have a path that is meant for you. How can you tell when you're on yours? By paying attention to how you

Chapter 1: The Pull

feel. When you are in your element, you feel great. And when you're not, you feel disconnected and unaligned. This feeling of disconnect is showing up to let you know you're in the wrong place. There is something better meant for you.

What do you love? What is something you're really good at that you feel your best when immersed in? That's it. That's your *Pull*. Whatever you feel called to do is the direction that is meant for you. It's that simple. *However, why the pull is there* is more complex, and we'll discuss this later. If your pull is so simple, why is it so hard to follow?

Human nature. It's human nature to instinctively protect yourself. This can sometimes show up as not being your true self or not being true *to* yourself. When you are in your most pronounced protective state, you are afraid. However, unless you are in danger, if you are basing your decision on fear, it will always be the wrong decision. What if you could shift your perspective and become *superhuman?* What if you could override the inherent tendency that sometimes holds you back?

Fear: *an unpleasant emotion caused by the belief that someone or something is dangerous, likely to cause pain, or a threat.*

If fear is an emotion, and emotion is a state of mind, doesn't that mean you have the power to shift it? A shift in perspective can awaken dormant powers you already have within you. While it is human nature to feel human emotions, each of them from time to time, you can learn to have control over your mind and where it leads you.

It takes focus. You have the ability to focus and to choose what you focus on. Wherever you focus is where you will go. Good or bad, you succeed at what you focus on. If you're not convinced of this, think back to something you achieved that you're proud of. How did you do it? You focused on it. First, the goal occupied your mind. You thought about it increasingly. You then invested time, effort, and energy.

Equally, think of something that didn't work out. Maybe a relationship or a promotion you got passed over on. What was your process leading up to the result? Even if you invested time and prepared for and hoped for a positive outcome, try and remember back. What was your emotional state around the goal? Were you scared? Did you hope for the best while fearing or expecting the worst? Rather than acknowledging and facing the emotions that came up, did you try and distract yourself? There is your proof once again. You succeeded at what you focused on. Your focus was on the fear, or it was outside of your relationship, or it was not addressing an underlying issue. Maybe the promotion was ultimately not going to resolve a deeper issue that was trying to get your attention through your emotions. If you failed at your goal, you failed to uncover and resolve the real issue because your focus was not *on* the real issue.

Sound confusing? We will discuss this more, and by the end of the chapter, the concept will become clearer. If there is something you want to improve or change, your work is to change your perspective. It will take some training and practice, as does everything new to you. Let's get started.

You can become superhuman just by observing your emotions. When you feel the fear creeping in and attempting to take over, you can switch it by asking yourself these questions:

Chapter 1: The Pull

"What if ... it does work out? What if I can do it? What might that be like?"

Curiosity is a powerful secret weapon that only you can take from yourself.

When you feel *the pull,* maybe you ignore it—for fear that it won't work out, for fear that if you invest your time and energy into something when the result is not guaranteed, you might lose. What's the worst thing that can happen when you admit you want something and then later you don't get it? You risk being vulnerable. You risk letting others see that you are vulnerable. Is there any way to be certain, to know for sure that things will work out? There is certainty, and there is doubt. Aren't both states of mind?

Perhaps a successful outcome is a choice, a state of mind you can choose to adopt. You can choose to believe with certainty that it will work out. You can then decide to focus on this feeling, this belief. You can also choose to lead with doubt, fearing things won't work out. Your future *is* guaranteed. Doubt guarantees failure because your mindset influences your actions or inaction. If you're adopting doubt as your dominant mindset around what you want, consider shifting your perspective.

When I feel anxious and like I'm not succeeding at something, I ask myself this question: *"Have you been focusing on it?"*

If the answer is "no" then I tell myself: *"Okay, start focusing on it."* I instantly feel better, having readopted my positive mindset and having redirected my focus which then influences my actions. Wherever you focus is where you're going. Where do you want to go?

The Best Things Happen When You Have No Idea What's Happening Next

I don't like surprises. I like my routine. In fact, I love my routine. I relish my morning ritual, which usually starts well before the sun comes up. Three a.m. is my favorite hour, my time to create. I feel focused and peaceful, as if I'm the first one awake in the whole world. I feel possibility in the quiet hum of undisturbed energy.

After my morning meditation and some writing, I usually get in a workout, then it's back to work, and later on, a walk or some errands to get moving again. Then later, if I don't have any social engagements, I'm back to more of whatever I'm working on. I feel my best during full productivity days like this. A surprise vacation invokes anxiety for me. *Who's going to take care of my cat? Will I get my yoga in?* But surprises in life? That's a different thing.

I have always believed the best things happen when you have no idea what's next. When you shift your perspective from worry to curiosity and allow yourself to follow what's calling you, you can expect to be surprised. Alternatively, when you choose to stay focused down a path that doesn't feel right, yet you know what to expect, you guarantee where you will be tomorrow. One day you look up, and a decade has gone by. I believe you live many lifetimes. Whether you agree with me or not, I imagine you agree that this is your life, right now, today. What do you want to do with it?

That's it. Right there. Before going any further, give yourself a moment to focus on the first thought that just came to your mind before your second thought crept in. The first thought is likely in the direction that feels right, and fear was likely your second thought. You can choose which thought you focus on. What if, instead of choosing fear, you choose curiosity? Keep reading, and I will show you how. But first, I'll tell you a story about how I overcame fear.

Overcoming Anxiety

As far back as I can remember, I was scared. Apparently, before I was even old enough to tell my mother what was wrong, I was scared. My grandfather, who is now 95 in 2022, as I write this, loves to tell me this story. I must have been two or three years old, he says. My mother had extended family over. I'm not sure what the occasion was. And my grandfather, with whom I've always had a special connection, says I wouldn't stop crying. No one knew what was wrong, and no one could get me to stop crying. Finally, my grandfather asked my mother if he could take me for a ride. I cried in the car, tears streaming down my cheeks, as he tried to get me to tell him what was bothering me.

He suggested we go to a bakery. I cried as we stood in line, fresh deli cookies and cakes behind the glass. Our turn came, and we stepped up. My grandfather said to me, "Now you can have anything that you want, but you have to stop crying and tell the nice lady what you want." He said I straightened myself right up, stopped crying, and told her what I wanted. This is the part of the story where my grandpa gives a hearty laugh, slaps his knees, throws his head back, and says, "The power of cookies!"

My grandpa shared this story with me for the first time only a few years back, many years after I had overcome two decades of chronic panic attacks. Panic is defined as *"sudden uncontrollable fear or anxiety."* When the attacks would escalate, I would find myself drenched in a cold sweat. Sometimes I would throw up or even appear to be having a seizure before I would ultimately lose consciousness. I have probably fainted a hundred times in my life. My grandfather later assessed I likely had a panic attack that day when the cookies came to my rescue. The attacks would follow me well into adulthood.

If you've never had a panic attack, I'll describe what it felt like for me. You know that ping of nervousness that pricks you when you're startled? It feels like a bad butterfly just before it drops into your stomach and begins its sinking decent. Imagine a hundred bad butterflies that never sink but instead fire every nerve in your body like little bolts of electricity. Imagine your heart pounding faster and faster, and then slowing down to big audible thuds. Imagine you're no longer inside yourself but just outside yourself, listening to the thuds.

Then the dizziness starts, the thuds fading as your blood pressure drops. You feel weak. You lie down, flailing your limbs in panic, grasping for some sense of control. A wave of nausea comes over you. You're getting hot. A moment later, you're lying in a pool of sweat. Becoming weaker, you lose the battle. You've lost control. The next thing you remember is waking up, hot and cold at the same time, weak yet now alert, and with several frantic people standing over you talking in loud voices. The smell of alcohol wafts under your nose as a nurse attempts to wake you back to consciousness, a little trick they use.

While to this day, I still get very nervous about things like medical procedures, including a routine blood draw, I no longer faint. I taught my mind to overcome the matter. The attacks used to be stimulated when I found myself in an environment that I could not get out of, where I felt trapped, like on a plane, for example. They also happened when I felt my boundaries were being crossed, like a doctor sticking a needle in my arm. The reason these attacks came on in the first place, I think, was due to my home environment growing up, where I had a lack of control. Even little ones need a sense of freedom, self-exploration, and the opportunity to begin understanding and establishing who they are. However, identifying the reason behind the attacks is not what ultimately cured them. Instead, I cured my panic attacks by changing my perspective, by choosing a different focus.

Often, you don't make a change until you see no other way, until you become uncomfortable enough. Discomfort, just like curiosity, can also be one of your greatest tools because when you're comfortable, you stay right where you are. But what if there is something better that is meant for you? This doesn't mean you can't ever be happy or content. But it does mean that you can let yourself get excited about greater things coming. You don't have to wait until you sink to your lowest low to begin lifting yourself up and getting curious about how things could be.

I did hit my lowest point before I began to heal my panic attacks. One day during my senior year in college, I became too scared to leave my apartment for fear that I might have a panic attack: agoraphobia. My big problem had gotten bigger. While the problem had been plaguing me my entire life, the thought didn't cross my mind that I might actually be able to change it until it became too big to continue dealing with. The time had come for me to choose a new mindset. I wanted to feel better. I chose to try. My new attitude quickly became a habit, which became a trait: perseverance. Not only would I try, but I would keep trying. I would admit to myself what it was I wanted, tell myself it was possible, and then inevitably, I would make it happen. I did it then, and have done it every day since with everything important enough for me to set my mind to. It's focus. I succeed at what I focus on. Now my focus is to help others do the same.

My attacks were getting progressively worse. While they were once stimulated by uncomfortable environments and situations, suddenly, they were happening in places I had once felt at ease, like my college classroom. When I felt my heart rate speeding up and that first little ping, I would escape to the bathroom. I learned that my biggest fear was not the thought of having a panic attack; it was having one *in front of people,* and a lecture hall filled with 70 of my classmates was certainly not ideal.

Once I was safely within the confines of the bathroom stall, I knew I would be okay because then, if it happened, no one would see. I would lay down on the cold tile floor and put my legs up, resting my feet on the door so the blood could flow back to my brain more easily. I don't think I ever once fainted in the bathroom stall. The fear had disappeared. I prevented the panic attacks by eliminating the fear. Fear is a state of mind, a perspective, which you have the power to shift. The end result of the panic attacks, fainting, *was* very real. But with a simple shift in my perspective, I changed my reality and ultimately I changed my life.

Fear can be debilitating. It doesn't get much more debilitating than falling unconscious. But I changed this pattern. I had anxiety attacks leading to fainting from when I was a little girl and into my twenties, and I changed the pattern. I shifted my perspective once I realized the attacks were being stimulated by fear. When I eliminated the fear, I was okay. I observed that when I was alone, the attacks would subside, and the worst of them didn't occur. I didn't faint. As I could get the attacks to subside when I was alone,

Chapter 1: The Pull

I began to think maybe I could do the same in public. I started to test my new theory.

When I felt the first sign of nervousness and my heart rate speeding up, I chose to shift my focus. I focused on breathing and the people around me. If I was talking with someone, I tried to focus completely on them, what they were saying, and how they looked. I focused outside of myself and on my external environment. I looked around and gave my full attention to whatever I was looking at. This new way of thinking took effort, concentration, and persistence, and ultimately it worked. I stopped fainting. I cured the attacks, and eventually, the fear that one might come on also went away.

Consider a perspective that might just change your life from this moment forward. If fear is an emotion based solely on what might or might not happen, wouldn't it be safe to say that fear is not real? How can it be real if it's based on "what if?" If fear can be so powerful that it can drive someone to lose consciousness, while no external physical harm is being done to their body, is it possible that a positive emotion can have the same degree of effect but in a positive way? I think it is, and I, along with countless others, have proven this theory.

Throughout the book, I will provide real-life stories and examples of proof, what I like to call my "science experiments." I'm not a scientist, and I'm not even good at science. But it's interesting and exciting that the theories I've learned and implemented throughout my life on my own, I now hear others speak on—professionals, including psychologists, psychiatrists, PhDs, and neuroscientists.

What if, when you begin thinking about the thing that you want, instead of focusing on the emotion of fear—fear that it might not work, fear that you can't—you instead conjure up the emotions of bliss, excitement, momentum, and certainty—certainty that it will work out? If fear can drive you to defeat, then couldn't belief in yourself drive you to success?

Overcoming is Becoming

Another theory I have is that your pain can actually be your catalyst when you choose to let it. It is often through your most painful experiences that you are driven to your calling. When you do the work to overcome your deeper challenges, you become equipped to live out your life's purpose in a way you otherwise would not have been prepared for. If you didn't endure whatever you went through, you likely would not feel compelled to do what was meant for you all along. An oyster only creates a pearl when its flesh is agitated. Diamonds are formed only under force and pressure. Through intense disruption, something happens. Discomfort stimulates growth, pushing you to new limits.

When you get uncomfortable enough, you make a change. You quit your job to pursue what you really want. You move into a new apartment, a space where you feel happier and freer. You stop talking to the friend who's negative and discouraging. You stand up for yourself. Often you don't acknowledge the problem until it has grown big enough. Only then do you create change. Problems are surface-level symptoms of the deeper underlying issue. Without problems, you would never address what's trying to get your attention. Wouldn't it make sense that the bigger the problem, the greater the impact of overcoming it?

Your pain can be the very tool in helping you become your best, or it can drag you down and keep you down. It's a choice. It's where you choose to focus your attention. It's from which view you angle your perspective. It's from which vantage you choose to perceive the world. The life you create for yourself is dictated by the choices you make each day. To uncover and live out the greatness within you, you must pay attention and listen to the pull, to what you feel drawn to. You must also listen and pay attention to what is bringing you pain so that you can overcome it and heal. Following the pull and being brave enough to listen to yourself is key in showing up as your best self, both for you and those around you.

In the next chapter, you will learn how to use your painful and uncomfortable experiences not only as tools to excavate the core challenges holding you back in one or more areas of your life, but also to funnel your frustration into the momentum-driven focus that is naturally within you, like a fossil fuel that has yet to be discovered. Are you ready to tap into yours?

Before moving on to the next chapter, take a moment to consider your *pull* with the chapter exercise below. You will be ready to move on to Chapter Two only once you've completed this exercise. This book is not just my story of what has worked for me; it is to be an interactive experience to help you uncover and overcome as well. Take the journey with me.

Chapter 1 Exercise: Identify Your *Pull*

Find a quiet space and give yourself fifteen or twenty minutes to sit and breathe. Yes, I am asking you to meditate. I'll share with you how I do it here, and once you begin to settle in and get more comfortable with practicing meditation, you will naturally create your own. There are also many resources online you can research to find a process that most resonates with you. Maybe at first, you begin with five minutes, and it later grows to 45 minutes. I now meditate each morning for 45 minutes to an hour. For this exercise, as you will be searching for something specific, I recommend aiming for 15 minutes.

With your eyes closed and taking in slow deep breaths, let yourself feel what it feels like to get present. Focus on what you hear. Birds chirping? A car horn in the distance? The hum of the air conditioner? Keep breathing as you take in the sounds. When your mind wanders off creating a narrative around the sounds you hear or bringing you back to your agenda for the day, take control back over your mind by focusing your attention back to your breath. No judgment.

As your mind drifts, just observe your focus and bring it back. Once your mind is calm, and you find yourself in the moment and not thinking back to something you could have done differently or what you need to do later, ask yourself a question:

"If I could do anything, anything in the world, and money was not an issue, and failure were not possible, what would I do?"

Before the second thought comes in, what would you do if you could do anything? Because that second thought will likely be fueled by fear:

"What if ... it doesn't work out? What if I can't?"

Well, what if it does, and what if you can? What if you could? Just think about that for this exercise, and we'll tackle the fear in the next chapter. You're here because somewhere inside of you,

you know you can. Or because you're curious. Curiosity leads to creation. Good job.

Master Your Mindset

1. Begin to take notice when you get a new idea. What is your emotion around the idea? Excitement?

2. If fear later creeps in, observe it and choose to focus back on the feeling of excitement.

3. Adopt the mantra: *What if it does work out?*

Some Extra Encouragement ...

If you don't yet know that you can, *I* know you can. Do you think I am capable of doing whatever I set my mind to? If you answered yes, and I already told you that I believe in you, and you just admitted that you believe in me, doesn't that mean that you believe in you? That was not meant to be a riddle, just the truth.

Now that you've discovered your pull, you're going to explore how to use your most painful experiences to gain wisdom instead of stress.

Chapter Two

The Catalyst

Chapter 2: The Catalyst

Your Deepest Pain Fuels Your Greatest Purpose

"Stress is an opportunity to show what you can do."
~Noel Medina

If you look for them, you will find stories of diamonds formed from pressure are not only within you; they are all around you.

One of the many things Oprah Winfrey is famous for is getting people to open up and talk about the abuse they suffered. In her documentary, *The Me You Can't See,* she opens up about the abuse she endured growing up. She talks about how her painful experiences have been a catalyst driving her to become who she now is.

"My life gets better when I think I can help other people in any way," she says. "I've sort of spent a career, a lifetime, a purpose doing that," she said. Oprah says she's grateful for her experiences, all of them. "It is because I was sexually abused, raped, that I have such empathy for people who've experienced that," she said. In another interview, she said, "You can use all of these things—experiences, good and bad in your life—to allow you to have post-traumatic wisdom instead of stress about it."

Her perspective is her choice. Oprah is reported to be worth $3.5 billion.[1] You can choose to focus on what you've learned, your wisdom that perhaps came from a negative or even unspeakable experience. Or you can keep your focus on the uncomfortable emotion stimulated by your painful experiences. You can't change your past, but you can choose to create a more desirable future.

Dwayne "The Rock" Johnson, arguably one of the manliest men on the planet, is open about his former battle with depression. While now worth $800 million, he grew up in poverty and talked about watching his mother attempt suicide.[2,3] He says, "I've learned over time to accept that vulnerability is a universal part of the human experience." Personally, I believe your greatest strength lies in vulnerability, and it looks like this strong man agrees.

Nelson Mandela served a 27-year prison sentence in his fight against apartheid, South Africa's racial class system of white supremacy.[4] While he was always a leader and a fighter, after

---

[1] "Oprah Winfrey Net Worth," Celebrity Net Worth, August 2, 2021, https://www.celebritynetworth.com/richest-celebrities/actors/oprah-net-worth/.
[2] "The Rock Dwayne Johnson Net Worth," Celebrity Net Worth, May 2, 2022, https://www.celebritynetworth.com/richest-athletes/wrestlers/the-rock-net-worth/.
[3] Philip Ellis, "The Rock Opened up about the First Time He Sought Help for Depression," Men's Health (Men's Health, November 2, 2021), https://www.menshealth.com/entertainment/a36853412/the-rock-depression-getting-help.
[4] "Nelson Mandela Released from Prison," History.com (A&E Television Networks, February 9, 2010), https://www.history.com/this-day-in-history/nelson-mandela-released-from-prison.

Chapter 2: The Catalyst

enduring this sentence, he later became an even more impactful leader—the first democratically elected president of South Africa.

Dr. Joe Dispenza, researcher, lecturer, and author, took a very big and very uncomfortable turn in his life that led to helping probably millions of people, including myself. He was living what sounds like a great life in Southern California. Running a successful chiropractic practice, he was also an avid athlete—practicing yoga, martial arts, and competing in triathlons. During one triathlon, he was hit by a truck and thrown from his bike, severely damaging his spine. He was deemed by four surgeons unlikely to walk again.[5]

He lay face down in a hospital bed for eight weeks, his doctors adamantly recommending surgery and even a full-body cast. Knowing that if he had the spine surgery, his range of motion would be severely limited, he began to think about healing his body in another way—through his mind. His thoughts ultimately led to his complete recovery. Eight weeks later, he was up walking around, and only ten weeks after his accident, he was back at work. This horrendous setback changed his life and later led him to change the lives of countless others.

Dr. Dispenza sold his chiropractic practice and began his quest for knowledge around other occurrences of spontaneous remission. He began researching and studying the common denominator among people who had healed their stage four cancer, blindness, MS, and other diseases. The common factor he discovered was in

---

[5] Dr. Joe Dispenza, "How I Healed Myself after Breaking 6 Vertebrae," The Placebo Effect - How I Healed Myself After Breaking 6 Vertebrae - Dr. Joe Dispenza (Heal Your Life, May 23, 2014), https://www.healyourlife.com/how-i-healed-myself-after-breaking-6-vertebrae.

their minds, within the brain. He now devotes his life to this research and teaching others how to heal themselves. I would wager the accident was Dr. Joe's most painful and challenging life experience. But, it is also the catalyst that led him to live out the greatness he might not have discovered otherwise.

Your Actions Under Pressure Dictate Your Life

My pull has always been toward freedom, self-expression, and helping others through my self-expression. Growing up, I endured the opposite. I'm a middle child, and I'd say I fit the mold, at least the part of *middle-child syndrome* that encompasses a strong desire for fairness, not just for oneself but everyone.[6] From the time I was very young, if I felt something wasn't right, I would speak up. I was the one in the family who challenged and pushed the limits, and my role in the family dynamic became "the problem."

It's easier to go along with things that don't feel right than it is to stand up and say, "No. This isn't right," especially when you're standing on your own. It's even harder when you get reprimanded for it. I have learned that sometimes when you feel disturbed by qualities in another, it's because you would like to possess that quality yourself. You try to minimize it because looking at it forces you to look in the mirror. There is something you could do better. Admitting you actually admire this other person's quality you put down, is admitting you have some work to do within yourself.

Although she has never said so, I believe this is my mother's issue with me. I think something about seeing her tiny little

---

[6] "Middle-Child Syndrome: The Effects of Birth Order on Character Traits," WebMD (WebMD, October 25, 2021), https://www.webmd.com/mental-health/what-to-know-middle-child-syndrome.

daughter boldly, and sometimes defiantly, standing up for herself and others since kindergarten age somehow made her feel small. Her apparent coping mechanism was to try and make *me* feel small.

As a kid, I was constantly in trouble, even though I was adamant (and still am) that I did nothing wrong. I got into trouble for speaking up, talking back, and expressing myself and was often trapped in my room as a result. When punished, I was ostracized from the family, only allowed out of my room to go to school and clean the house. So while my mom, stepdad, brother, and sister were downstairs watching a favorite TV show after dinner, I was in my room by myself. When I would venture down the hall to talk with my little brother, whom I adored, my stepdad's voice bellowed at me from downstairs to get back in my room.

I felt unaccepted by the people who were supposed to love and accept me no matter what. During the impressionable years when I was trying to understand and assert myself and shape how I felt about myself, I learned that I was unlovable and should be ignored. I learned that expressing myself would have consequences and that if I didn't ask for love and often, even beg for it, I would not get it.

I was developing a detrimental pattern that would hold me back in important areas of my life for decades to come. But I made a choice, even though, at the time, I was too young to understand the positive mindset I was choosing. I chose to focus on what I *did* have control over and to control what I could. I could not control that my mother often ignored me unless she was yelling at me. I could not control that my stepfather rolled his eyes at me and grounded me when I stood up for myself. Each time I uttered, "But …" one week in my room became two.

While it's a sad story, my story is also part of what made me who I am. Had I not been stifled and confined, I would not have the strong push I do toward freedom. Had I not been punished for speaking up, I probably would not feel the strong pull to express myself.

Mindset Influences Choices. Choices Dictate your Future.

You can choose to let your negative circumstances frame your state of mind. Or you can choose to get curious about how you can get yourself feeling better. Writing was the first positive choice I made for myself out of a negative circumstance. I was about 11 years old.

The more my parents tried to keep me from expressing myself, the stronger my drive became. How could I express myself while alone in my room, staring out the window at my friends playing across the street? What *did* I have control over? I could write. I had a journal, and so I began writing. Inside my room and unable to talk with anyone, I found a way to express myself for weeks and sometimes months at a time. Not only did I keep my self-expression in this way, I expanded it.

I started with poetry. I liked words, and I liked making them rhyme. I wrote tons of poems when I was little. Occasionally I'll write one now but not very often because, for me, poetry was just for when I was feeling sad. While I was sad for many years, even into my thirties, I'm not sad much of the time anymore. I have ups and downs like everyone, but the overall state of mind I come back to each day is happy, inspired, and excited.

Speaking up, talking back, and pushing the limits are things kids naturally do when becoming who they are. They are learning to assert themselves, so they later know how to as adults. Not being allowed this as a child only increased my desire. Even as a very young girl, I knew I had something to say. It may have taken me many years to get where I was going, but I was on the path. And with each positive choice I made for myself, I took another step in the right direction, the one that was meant for me all along.

What I went through as a child fueled my drive to help others feel better faster. I became an author, a speaker, and a very assertive woman in general, despite my stifled upbringing, or maybe because of it. I still found a way to become myself. No one can make you not who you are. You are who you are. The quicker you learn to be 100% yourself, the happier you become and the better experiences you attract.

In keeping with my increasing pull toward freedom, the second positive choice I made for myself was to take up running. I started running at twelve years old. I wasn't allowed to do much, but I was allowed to go running. I remember my first run. I was in the yard with my family; I guess I was not in trouble that day. I looked down the street and, feeling a sudden burst of energy, I wanted to run down to the neighborhood entrance and back. I asked my parents if I could, and they said, "Yes." I took off. It was 800 yards of freedom, and I liked it. When I got back, I asked if I could go again.

I had found a way to create some freedom for myself. That 800 yards would later become one mile and then two, up to five, six, and sometimes even 10 miles or more. Still, today when I am running, I feel happy and free. Had I not felt the strong desire for freedom, or to escape, I may not be a runner today. Back then, it was an escape, and today it's a place to feel good, celebrate myself and my freedom, think about my goals, and keep pushing myself. It still feels amazing.

My inherent push for freedom also manifested as a path to my independence. As a kid, I couldn't wait to start working. Work was an outlet where I could begin to exhaust some of my endless energy. I poured everything into my work. I did a good job, and I didn't get into trouble. That felt really good, and I developed a strong work ethic from a young age—another positive choice out of negative circumstances. And with each job I chose, I continued moving toward greater freedom. Today I work for myself. The pull for me is still all about freedom and self-expression. And in continuing to surrender to and follow the pull, stimulated by pain, I am aligning with what is meant for me.

I'm grateful for the experiences I recognize as catalysts toward the life I created. I bet the same is true for you, that your painful experiences pushed you onto and further down the path meant for you. You have the power to make healthy choices for yourself despite your painful experiences. You'll know which choices are right by listening to the pull, to what you are being drawn to.

Discomfort Is a Great Thing

It's easy to stay uncomfortable because at least you know what to expect. But what happens when you get squeezed tighter, and the pressure becomes too much? You begin to get curious about how things *could* be. You begin to wonder, *"What if?"* This curiosity, often stimulated by discomfort, shows up to help you follow your pull.

Looking back throughout my life, each impactful change began with discomfort. While sometimes you may be uncomfortable for years, you often don't make a change until things get worse. *Tower moments*—very uncomfortable events that force change—can occur when we're not making the change we need to. Your problems get bigger so you pay them some attention and change course. When you still don't, the Universe steps in and does it for you. Tower moments are often quite painful, however necessary, to get you on track, the track that is meant for you. Dr. Joe's accident was likely a tower moment. Although it sounds like he was leading a happy and fulfilling life, one in which he was helping his chiropractic patients, there was a greater impact for him to make.

Take a moment now to look back over your life and consider the times when you made an impactful change. How did you feel just before you made the change? Likely, you felt frustrated; you felt uncomfortable. Now look back further. How long had you actually been feeling uncomfortable before you decided to do something about it? When the problem became too big to ignore, suddenly it had your attention. But you don't have to wait until you are extremely uncomfortable before making a change. Instead, you can learn to pay attention to how you're feeling, choose a different perspective, and ultimately improve your life faster. We will discuss this more later in the book.

Before I decided to go into business for myself, I was uncomfortable. Looking back, I had been unhappy for a long time. That unhappiness was trying to get my attention, but it didn't until it grew bigger. I was so busy with work that I just kept my head down, often working ten and sometimes twelve-hour days. My mood was negative, which affected my demeanor, which affected my interactions with people, which surely limited opportunities. I just thought being short-tempered was my personality. It was becoming my personality, but it's not who I am. Finally, something got my attention—a triggering event. I became so frustrated during a conversation with my boss that I wanted to quit that instant. Instead, I paused. I gave myself a moment to sit with the discomfort and let myself observe it.

When you take a step outside yourself and objectively observe your emotions and reactions, you're able to see something you didn't before. This shift in perspective can quickly bring a solution to your problem – a problem you perhaps didn't notice before. An answer you didn't know you were looking for is suddenly staring you in the face. Your new path becomes clear, and you instantly trust it.

When you try to ignore your emotions, you're not present. Getting present sometimes means sitting with how you're feeling and letting your emotions exist. When you take the pressure off of trying to ignore your discomfort, you can uncover the real problem. You only discover the solution once you see the problem. I had been going on in a state of discomfort for a few years by this time. But I wasn't uncomfortable *enough*. The Universe made my problems even bigger until I realized I had to move.

While the discomfort took years to build before I was finally ready to do something about it, the answer showed up in seconds, but only once I observed my emotions and allowed myself to get curious about *"What if?"* There would be more brainstorming, researching, risk assessing, and planning. But three weeks later, I had transitioned to working for myself.

Another time I got a big nudge from the Universe was just before I moved to New York. While this tower moment was not a painful one for me, the experiences leading up to it were. Still, I had not made the necessary changes. It was time for the Universe to step in and force its hand. I was 31 years old and had wanted to move to New York since I was eight. Getting a job, an apartment, and enough money to move to New York is not the easiest thing in the world, but it's certainly not impossible, although many people told me it was. At this time in my life, I was feeling disconnected and unfulfilled. I'd started my sales career, and a few years in, I was doing fine, but I felt no real connection to my work or to the people I spent time with. I needed a new environment, one where I felt stimulated and more like myself.

My entire life, since I was little, I had carried this emotion of frustration around with me. It was unspent energy. Living in Manhattan requires a lot of energy. While I had always inherently known New York was the place for me, there I was, in my thirties and making no strides to get here. The tower moment that happened was I lost my job. The company sold, and everyone was laid off.

I actually felt happy. There was my sign. It was time. I began applying for jobs in New York, and two months later, I landed one and moved here. I'd had it in me all along. But it wasn't until I got uncomfortable enough, and then lost my job, that I decided to create change. Moving to New York was the best decision I've ever made for myself. I have made some other great decisions since, but getting to New York put me on my path. I was unhappy, and I picked myself up and put myself in a place where I felt at home. I still had a ways to go. However, I became ten times happier overnight, but not until I got uncomfortable enough to make a change.

Another positive decision I made for myself out of discomfort was when I was fifteen years old. I had been growing increasingly miserable in my homelife, and I likely could have asked to move into my dad's house in the midwest years before, but I didn't—not until I found myself sinking into a deeper depression. I had been an honor roll student, and with things at home getting worse, I was now getting D's. My self-esteem sunk so low that at field hockey practice, I sat on the bench with my head in my hands rather than asking to get in the game. Even then, I knew that if I didn't do something about my situation, I'd be heading off to college with zero self-confidence.

Finally, I called my dad. I still remember sitting on my bed, enduring another two-week-long sentence of being confined to my room. I picked up the phone. A couple of rings later, my dad answered.

"Can I come live with you?" I said.

He said, "Yes."

I moved there after two weeks. And just like that, I changed my life. Of course, it wasn't all roses after that, but it was a start and a much better environment for me to begin rebuilding my self-confidence before starting college.

Creating change begins with paying attention to your emotions and then letting yourself sit with them and seeing what comes up. It is uncomfortable to sit with your discomfort, but you're already uncomfortable. And if you're uncomfortable enough to notice, chances are you've been uncomfortable for a long time. Feeling your feelings, exploring them more deeply, and getting curious about them, takes some pressure off. It's okay to feel the way you do. And more importantly, acknowledging and accepting your feelings brings you present. The present moment is the only place where something can happen, including change. The present moment is where the ideas come.

Looking back throughout your life, I'm confident you will notice that you have already implemented this tactic, creating change when you're uncomfortable, thousands of times. How many meals have you had? When you got uncomfortable enough, you got up and made yourself something to eat. When your bladder got full enough, you excused yourself to the bathroom. You didn't get up and go when you first noticed the urge, when it was a mild discomfort. You dismissed it and kept doing what you were focused on. Although the urge was there, you didn't choose to do something about it until the discomfort grew bigger. Then you made a change, and then you felt relief. You felt better. You can do this with anything you set your mind to. The difference is that you've made yourself a meal and used the bathroom enough times to know what to expect. Because you're not afraid of the outcome, you just do it, now mechanically.

Ever changed jobs or moved into a new apartment? Something made you uncomfortable enough to make a change. Once you create change and have a positive outcome, you become more comfortable leaning into the discomfort instead of avoiding it. You begin to trust yourself and your instincts. You can adopt a new habit of listening to yourself, feeling your emotions and getting curious about them, letting them guide you in the right direction, and following your pull.

The best thing you can do when you're feeling uncomfortable is to allow yourself to feel your feelings. Rather than try and avoid them with a distraction to feel better, sit with the discomfort and see what comes up. It is your pain that pushes you. If you're uncomfortable, there's a reason. Change is needed. And if you're brave enough, change is coming, which means you have something to get excited about.

The impact of this last step, getting excited, is life-changing. In the next chapter, we'll go deeper into simple steps you can take every day to become a mega-manifester, raising your state of general happiness. Once you do this, while you will have ups and downs and some days will be better than others, your overall state of mind and state of being will never drop below the level you have raised it to. And if it does, you just implement one or more of the tools we'll continue discussing to quickly pick yourself back up. Creating change is just like learning anything new; it takes telling yourself you can and then trying and continuing to try. Tell yourself you can because you can. Then try, and keep trying.

Chapter 2 Exercise: Identify Your Outcome Choices

Before moving on to the next chapter, complete the chapter exercise to instill your confidence by establishing proof in the process.

Consider a time when you set a goal and accomplished it. What was the goal? How did you first get the idea? Were you frustrated with the current state of things? What was your process in reaching your goal, and what was the outcome? What was the emotion fueling your path to success? Write down your answers.

Now think of something you're unsatisfied with in your life, something you feel unhappy thinking about. Have you tried working on this issue in the past? If so, what was your goal, your process, and the emotion you carried behind it? Write down your answers.

Master Your Mindset

1. When dealing with uncomfortable circumstances, make a choice to invest in yourself. What activity can you do to better yourself or to make yourself feel a little better?

2. When feeling frustrated, sit with the discomfort and observe it to ultimately uncover and address the real problem.

Some Extra Encouragement ...

After completing the chapter exercise, you will likely see that your outcomes are choices. Choose to keep reading, and the process of creating change will get easier, later becoming second nature.

Now that you've identified your outcome choices, it's time to let go of some control. I'll show you how and tell you why this is useful in Chapter Three.

Chapter Three

The Quest

Chapter 3: The Quest

Let Go, Allow, and Surrender

"The moment of surrender is not when life is over; it's when it begins."
~Marianne Williamson, Author

If there ever were a pot calling a kettle black, it would be the subtitle of this chapter. I'm a doer, an achiever, a go and getter. I make things happen. What sort of things? All things, except for those I have no control over. Therein lies the problem, which took me a long time to figure out.

Getting what I wanted has worked quite well for me, except for the areas in which it didn't. In those areas, doing, achieving, and going and getting was not the way. So if I were ever going to receive in the areas that weren't working in my life, I was going to have to learn to relinquish control and let go.

While I was physically safe in my environment growing up, emotionally, I felt unsafe. I learned from a very young age that I had to rely on myself to keep myself protected. Self-reliance is a beautiful strength, but as your good qualities often can, this strength held me back in some areas. With each step down the path of self-exploration, I fill in another piece of the puzzle—why I am the way that I am, why some things hurt so much, why I react the way I do, and why I struggle in certain areas. This deeper understanding of myself helps me create change for myself and to better understand others.

The need to force or control is fear-based. It's lacking the ability to trust that it will come, whatever *it* is for you and for me. My whole life, I've worked to control what I can—my career, the money I make, the things I accomplish, my fitness. When I'm ready for change and searching for a solution, once I uncover it, I spring into action. See target, hit target. And when I don't yet have the answer, I trust that it will come. It always does, and my life gets richer and better—except for in one area.

While I was abundant in career success and on track with my life purpose goals, love was another story. The lack of love in my life was something I couldn't control. Knowing this, I did what I felt were the right things. I focused on my work and my passions, continuously investing in myself. I wasn't looking for it, so why wasn't it coming?

When I thought I saw it coming in, I would get excited. But then, when the guy wasn't doing what I wanted or needed, I would, true to form, spring into action and try to control the situation. Instead of letting go, the obvious answer, I would begin doing all of the doing myself. It took me years to learn that this doesn't work, as a relationship is a partnership with two investors. Taking on the role of the primary investor was a pattern that left me feeling empty.

If I could let go, allow, and surrender in other areas of my life, and as a result, things happened for me, turning out just as I had wanted and with ease, why not in this area? The *why* was the problem. I didn't understand why. How could I fix this issue when I didn't understand it?

The quest for self-improvement will forever be ongoing. But along the way, you stumble across the answers you're searching for, as long as you're on your path, as long as you decide to start and then keep going. Once you choose to begin your quest, you will eventually uncover the underlying issue and then discover the solution. The process can often be painful, but it works. Let your curiosity guide you to the next puzzle piece, and as the beautiful picture of your true self unfolds, you will receive more and with greater ease.

Curiosity Is Underrated

Curiosity: *a strong desire to know or learn something.*

I've never done well with gray areas. While others may be able to get going with limited information, I need all the details. This quality satisfies my theory that your best qualities are often one and the same as your worst, or at least there is some good in your "perceived" bad qualities. Similarly, your good qualities can sometimes hold you back. For example, I'm thorough and detail-oriented. This makes me a great writer, an innate understander of people, and great at my job. But the other side of this strong quality is the need to control.

I encourage you to play a little game of identifying your best and supposed worst qualities and see if they are, in fact, one and the same. I think it's a nice self-esteem booster helping you to be a little easier on yourself and extend some self-love. We'll take a moment to do this at the end of this chapter.

As an adult, I now have the ability to control my environment. I want to make sure I am comfortable. This is not necessarily a bad thing. If I don't have enough details to feel confident that I'll have a good time and be comfortable in a situation, I'm not going, even if I've previously committed myself. If something is unclear in my head, I have pause. My wheels begin turning as I try to formulate my questions. This is likely one reason I'm a big do-it-yourselfer. I want to fully understand how to do it myself before passing it off to someone else, which sometimes helps, and other times hinders.

While keeping myself comfortable is empowering, in other ways, it can be limiting. The Law of Attraction is a powerful force that is constantly at play, and while man has no control over the Law of Attraction, of its existence or power, *every* man has the ability to sway this law to work for him. You are only eligible to win the game when you play by the rules. And when you play by the rules, doesn't life go easier on you? The Law of Attraction is more than just positive thinking. The key is the *emotion* you're carrying in association *with* your thoughts. You attract more of how you feel. For good and for bad, the Law of Attraction is at work. When it's working against you, you live your life as a victim.

I first learned about the Law of Attraction years ago when I watched the movie *The Secret*. But I actually believe I've been practicing the concept since I was much younger. Whenever I thought about something I wanted to do or achieve, I always believed I could. I saw myself doing it in my mind, and then I took it further by getting excited about it. And if I fell, I never really saw it as a failure. I just tried again. I got the thought to start running, I saw myself doing it, and I got started, later becoming a long-distance runner. While a great workout, to me, it now feels effortless—an achievement that started with an idea, then a vision, then excitement around the idea, and then perseverance.

Once I got started in my career, I wanted to make more money and saw myself making more money. I didn't know how the opportunities would come or exactly what I'd be doing; I just knew that I would be successful. But I took it a step further without consciously realizing at the time what I was doing. And this is the key. I got *excited* about it. In thinking about what I wanted, I also conjured up the emotion of how I would feel, as if it were happening at that moment. While a lot of people will say, "I don't want to get my hopes up," I'm always busy getting my hopes up. I'm always excited about what I'm working on and what I'm working toward, enjoying the process while feeling as though I'm already there. I expect to create greatness, and so I do.

The Life-Changing Life-Creating Process

Anyone can change their life in a matter of seconds. While you may take many challenging steps to get where you're going, establishing the foundation that ultimately brings you what you want takes seconds.

When a thought or idea pops into your mind, the first step is to acknowledge it. Let it exist. This thought came into your mind at a moment when you were present, without fear of what might or might not happen, and with no time to think about what didn't work out in the past. The present is the only place where you can create. Doesn't it make sense then that your creative ideas come when you are present? And it also makes sense that when you are feeling down, sad, or regretful of the past, you cannot create positive outcomes for yourself. When you are thinking in terms of the past, you are keeping yourself stuck.

By focusing on a negative past emotion, you are missing potential opportunities. The same is true when you worry about the future. What's the emotion behind worry? Fear. Anytime you're fearful, you're not feeling good. You're not present; therefore, you cannot create. Conclusion? Trust the present moment. Trust your thoughts and ideas that come to you when you are present. Feel the glimmer of excitement around your idea and trust the dream is there for a reason. That's step number one. Acknowledge your idea.

Once you've acknowledged your idea, step two is to let your idea exist. Sit with your idea and let it expand. When human nature creeps in, which happens equally as fast, your next job is to push the negative thought away. Just as fast as the fear-based questions come in, push them aside. Override the *What if I can't?* with *What if I can?* Instead of worry, choose to focus on a different emotion. This part will be an uncomfortable challenge at first if it's new to you. Believe it or not, what you choose to think *is* a choice. You have the power to choose what you focus on. Choose excitement. Like anything you diligently practice, it gets easier and, pretty soon, becomes your nature. This is step number three: get excited.

Step number four is to get curious. Wonder is a powerful tool. Think about the thing that you want to do or achieve. Then, envision yourself doing it and let wonder take over. "I wonder what that might be like." And when worry tries to creep in again, *How is this going to work?* replace it with curiosity. "I *wonder* how this *will* work out." Keep repeating the process.

When you have to know *how* something will work out, you can stop yourself from ever getting started. When I get excited about a new project or venture and share my idea with friends, they will sometimes ask me *how* I'm going to do it. I make it a practice not to answer this question. They don't need to know how because *I* don't need to know how. I just have to start.

This is step number five. Get started. But the first four steps, the foundation of a winning mindset, occur within just seconds. You can change your life in seconds just by changing your mind. You can't possibly know what your path will look like and who you will meet to help you on your way. This is a good thing because if you could, you would surely limit yourself.

Steps to the Life-Changing Life-Creating Process

1. Acknowledge your idea.

2. Let your idea exist. Sit with it. Let it expand.

3. Get excited. Push fear aside and focus on your excitement.

4. Get curious. Focus on what it will *feel* like to succeed.

5. Get started. This means get present with an activity – work, fun, whatever comes up. Your first step in actually *getting started* toward your goal, will show up.

When you try to control your future, making your decisions around avoiding risk, pain, or the potential to fail, you do fail, because you don't try.

When you stay present, you are open. This is the letting go, allowing, and surrendering, trusting that your next step will show up. It is in these moments the ideas come, that the Universe speaks to you. It is up to you to continue staying present by holding onto the idea and then taking it further by getting excited. When fear comes in, you are no longer in the present moment. You are in the future. You are no longer manifesting. You are no longer creating. When you employ your ability to push past the fear and instead choose the emotion of excitement, you become superhuman. You become manifesters, and when you keep going and growing in this direction, you become mega-manifesters.

Change Involves Changing Your Mind

Consider some of the greatest inventors of all time. Thomas Edison invented the lightbulb; Henry Ford invented the Model-T automobile. Alexander Graham Bell invented the telephone. Johannes Gutenberg invented the printing press. The Wright brothers invented flying. Grace Hopper pioneered computer programming, and neonatal nurse Sharone Ragone forever changed the standard of care for premature patients with her invention of medical devices designed specifically for babies.

Each of them first got an idea. Had they not allowed themselves to get curious about their idea and instead chose to focus on fear that it might not come to fruition, would they have achieved their dream? Your mind, imagination, and curiosity can be your most powerful tools when you allow your ideas to exist. When you begin to wonder what your dream will look like when it does work out, you are going the right way. Just as children are not afraid to daydream, get excited, or believe in what can be, neither are the most accomplished people in history.

While curiosity is a tool you can use, the need to know can keep you stuck. As a self-proclaimed "achiever," surrendering and allowing, versus controlling my life, has been one of my most challenging and important lessons. But I think I finally figured out the piece of my life that wasn't working. With the elements of my life that are going great, I listen to my instincts and employ curiosity and wonder. While I didn't realize it at the time, I was letting go, surrendering, and trusting that my first step would show up. This mindset and these actions then allow the first step to show up. Each time, it has. When it does, I'm ready to hop into my achiever mode, the part of myself that helps me get things done. My ability to let life point me in the direction that is ultimately meant for me helps me achieve with less effort. For the parts of my life that were not going in my favor, the solution was to simply apply the same concept.

Stay Present and Take the First Step

If you're walking down the street and focusing two blocks ahead, aren't you likely to miss what's right in front of you? Achieving your dreams is no different. When you are worried about or focused on steps eight, nine, and ten, how can you allow the first step to show up? Even when it's right in front of you, you won't see it.

Getting started is the hardest part, but it only takes a moment. And typically, once you get started on a project, whether it's a chore or a workout or brainstorming on your new business venture, a few minutes in, you're immersed, invested, and building momentum.

My CPA had requested a tax document from me. While I'm pretty organized when it comes to things that are important to me, my *important papers* are not. While I might need some of them, I don't want them, nor do I find them interesting. As a result, I could certainly be more organized with my important papers.

While you do grow and change, your inherent tendencies can linger. I began compiling important papers with my first job back in high school. My dad gave me a purple file box to store them. Begrudgingly and disinterested, I put my important papers into the purple box. Say that five times out loud. They weren't exactly organized, but they were inside the box. And then, when I moved out, I left my important papers at my dad's house. I think he still has the purple box.

Today I have my important papers stored in several different locations, still not the most organized of systems. When my CPA requested an important document, it could have been in any one of my six important papers containers or piles. The last thing I wanted to do was look for it. But I had to. That Saturday morning, I started my search, and as soon as I got going, I gained some momentum and even enjoyed the process. Not only did I find the document in about ten minutes, but I also kept going until I'd re-organized all of my important papers, although I'm pretty sure they're still pretty unorganized.

Momentum is a beautiful thing that, again, starts with an idea. I get the idea to go for a run. The hardest part is getting started. Twenty minutes in, I feel like I'm flying. I pick up my pace and let it carry me effortlessly, and when it's time to stop, I feel like I could easily go another hour. Idea. Excitement. Curiosity. Heightened excitement. Getting started. Momentum. Repeat. And before you have time to even think about looking back, you have surprised yourself at just how far you've come. If you let yourself get caught up in *how* or *if* it will work out, you'll still be at the starting line. You cannot know what will happen next, and life's unpredictability is a gift. However, one thing is certain: when you go in the direction of what feels right, you are on your way.

Chapter 3: The Quest

I had known for about five years that I wanted to be a motivational speaker. The idea came to me, and I acknowledged its existence. I let my idea exist. This is very important. I didn't know how it would happen or when. But I knew that it would. I also knew it was not yet time. I wrote down my idea, and would later come back to it. On multiple other occasions, the idea came to my mind again, each time a little louder. And then, one day, it lingered longer than usual. It was time.

I remember thinking, "How is this going to happen? It's unlikely that someone is going to invite me to speak on something when I haven't done it before. I'll just get started." And I did. I set a goal of going live with my YouTube channel, where I would speak on topics that I find inspiring and thought would be helpful to others. I started writing down my ideas. I taught myself how to set up the channel and shoot and edit videos. And I got started.

I began shooting videos in the park a couple of times a week, and I really enjoyed it. It felt right. I didn't know what might come of it or how; I just knew I had some wisdom to share and that speaking on things I've learned and implemented felt good. One day I was shooting a video, and a guy walking by stopped and listened to what I was saying. My message resonated enough for him to stop and chat with me. He later found my website and sent me an email. We became friends.

Eric Lubitz was the first person to read and review my first book. He also connected me with his media contacts as he's a retired sportscaster. We now talk each week and go for walks on the East River on sunny days, during which we share lots of laughs and inspire creative ideas. Eric brings much joy to my life. How could I have ever predicted that would happen when I first set out to shoot a video? There's no way for you to know, and it's not your business to. But it is your responsibility to listen to what's calling your attention, get excited about it, and then stay present.

Give Yourself Moments

It's also your job to keep yourself feeling good; for that to happen, you must be present, and vice versa. You are not your most productive when feeling restless or uneasy. While attempting to force your focus in one direction, your distracted mind veers off in another. When you pay attention to what is calling you, even when it seems insignificant, you create room for new ideas and paths to show up. And here's a little secret: you can achieve more by doing more of what you feel like doing.

Productivity: *effectiveness of effort.*

How effective are you when you're focused and motivated? And what motivates you, what captures your attention? Something you feel like doing. You often have things you don't necessarily feel like doing but do have to get done. You can be more effective when you give in to what is calling your attention and run with that, just for a little bit.

As a self-proclaimed achiever, it can sometimes feel uncomfortable for me not to keep pushing myself when I need a break. But when I do keep pushing myself in one direction while my brain or body wants to go in another, I'm not my most productive. When I give myself what I need, whether it's a run, some time to write, a trip to my favorite store, or just to take a break and read a book or watch a movie, when I come back, I am 100% focused on whatever I need to work on, and I get it done much more efficiently, with less time and effort.

When you give yourself time to focus on what you need or want, you also signal to the Universe that you are ready for more of that. I call this giving yourself *moments* to focus on what you feel like. If you want more peace in your life yet never give yourself time to enjoy some peace in your life, like going for a walk in the sun, watching your favorite show, or spending time with a good friend, how can the Universe give you more of something you won't take? When you begin to take just a little time for yourself by focusing on what you feel like, more time begins to show up because you no longer have a distracted focus. You increase your motivation all around and have newfound energy for even necessary, yet mundane, tasks.

The year I generated the most revenue from my business was the same year I wrote and published my first book, the same year I posted more motivational videos than the year before, and the same year I started life coaching—all very time-consuming endeavors—yet I still got plenty of sleep and fit in regular workouts. In giving myself time to do more of what I felt like, I effortlessly increased my productivity when it came time to do what I needed to get done.

Remember to pay attention to how you're feeling. If you're feeling distracted, unfocused, or unsatisfied at the moment, ask yourself, *"What do I feel like doing?"* Give yourself moments to do more of what you feel like and watch the shift in your productivity. You might ultimately surprise yourself by discovering a new direction that was meant for you all along. Or you might just feel happier and more satisfied as you achieve more with less effort.

Chapter 3 Exercise: Identify and Do What You Feel

You guessed it. Take a moment to do what you feel like doing. Right now, what do you feel like doing? Consider adopting this new mindset and begin practicing taking time each day to spend focusing on something you feel called to do. You might discover a new direction, or you might just get yourself vibrating in a more positive energy. As you attract more of how you're feeling, doing what you feel like keeps you feeling good and turns the Law of Attraction in your favor.

Master Your Mindset

1. When you get a new idea or goal, choose wonder over worry.
2. Employ the life-changing, life-creating process: Acknowledge your idea. Let your idea exist and expand. Get excited. Get curious. Get started.
3. Surrender. Relinquish control. Allow the first step to show up rather than preventing yourself from seeing it.
4. Give yourself *moments* to do what you feel like.

Some Extra Encouragement ...

One little thing I enjoy doing is walking to TJ Maxx. It's a nice 20-minute walk in my neighborhood and a little gift I give myself. I might buy some vanilla-scented candles there. Maybe I'll buy nothing. Either way, I enjoy the trip. This time I give to myself when I feel called to is the gift of freedom, aligning me once again with my pull toward freedom. Doing what you feel like can be a little thing or a big thing. Just know that in doing it, you are signaling to the Universe that you are ready for more of that.

Whatever that is for you, are you ready to make it happen faster? In the next chapter, we'll talk about how.

Chapter Four

Becoming a Mega-Manifester

Chapter 4: Becoming a Mega-Manifester

You Always Want More. How Do You Get It?

> "Believe you can, and you're halfway there."
> ~*Theodore Roosevelt*

You've learned that the key to getting what you want begins with paying attention to your emotions. Once you uncover what it is you want and get started on the path in your new direction, how do you move further and faster down your path? You already know. The answer, once again, is in your emotions. Choose to focus on the uplifting, encouraging emotion of excitement. As many years as I've been working on myself, I still come to understand this concept more deeply every day. In this chapter, you will further explore the practice of conjuring up excitement by daydreaming. You will also learn how to turn what may have started as frustration into momentum-driven focus.

Focused Manifestations

I'm a morning person, always have been. And my mornings keep getting earlier and earlier. I sometimes wake up at 1 or 2 a.m. Occasionally I'll even wake up at midnight. When this happens, since I'm wide awake, I use the time. I start the coffee and get my day going. Does this make me nuts? Yes. You don't have to wake up at 3 a.m. to do your focused manifestations. You can do them any time of day. You can even come back to the emotion throughout your day. Ultimately, this is the goal, to be somewhat daydreaming and excited about where you're heading, all day long. We will explore this more later in the book.

Each morning I pour my first cup of French press black coffee into my favorite mug, unless it's in the dishwasher, in which case I pour my coffee into whichever runner-up favorite coffee mug is clean. But my favorite coffee mug is a souvenir my dad bought me from the Empire State Building gift shop. It's white with a stenciled view of the city skyline and a quote that says, "I always come back to Manhattan." I love this mug. With my giant cup filled with rich, black, steaming coffee, I walk over to my back door and peer outside. I look up into the dark sky, with usually just one or two stars still lingering. In Manhattan, most of the stars stay hidden, blending in with the city lights.

I've always loved looking up at the sky. I love the puffy white clouds that appear on a warm summer day. I love the clear periwinkle skies on a crisp fall day. I love tumultuous stormy skies, the clouds rolling in to relieve the humidity. Maybe my favorite sky is the undisturbed, midnight blue night sky, filled with the possibility of the unknown.

When I was little and visiting my dad in Kansas during the summer, one of my favorite things was to sit on the back deck with him at night and gaze up at the stars. Somehow, even though there were a lot of us kids with our blended family, I remember this time, just me and my dad. He would help me find the Big Dipper and the Milky Way. I was always in awe when looking up at the stars and still am.

Some things you keep with you, no matter how far away you move or how much you grow. Just like I still don't care about my important papers, I still love looking up at the sky. I suppose that's because I'm still a dreamer. My daydreaming as a little girl never stopped. For me, morning time is a time to dream, although I also dream throughout the day.

Sipping my coffee with my cat at my feet, I stare into the still night sky and think about the things I am grateful for. Even when I wake up feeling great, I always say to myself, "Time to get vibrating higher." I take time to think about maybe ten things I'm grateful for. I don't keep count; I just have to stop at a certain point as I'm brewing with momentum and excitement to get my day going. My official *day* starts with writing, but first, I manifest. First, I dream. You already know how to do this. You did it as a kid.

After practicing gratitude, I sit down on a pillow on the floor, or outside on my balcony if the weather is nice, coffee by my side and my cat, Gilligan, finding his way onto my lap. He's one of the things I'm grateful for. Then I begin my breathing exercises. Breathing exercises are said to extend your lifespan. In doing breathing exercises for just a few minutes each morning, I quickly noticed significant improvements.

The first thing I noticed was suddenly feeling the urge to sing more. I've never been a shower singer, but suddenly I was. I also noticed how much my voice had improved. Before, my breath would become shallow, and my vocal cords fatigued. Now I could carry the note as long as the artist in the song. My range also improved. Before, I was a one-note wonder, and now I have some range. The third thing I noticed was how much calmer I was in my

Bikram hot yoga classes. While I've been practicing yoga for 15 years, before, I would get tired, or my heart rate would become too elevated, and I'd come out of the pose early. Now I had no problem staying in the posture.

While the practice is always a challenge as you continue pushing yourself, balancing strength with flexibility, my mind was suddenly calm. The ability to remain calm in a challenging hot yoga class is the ability to remain calm in challenging situations in life. Breathing just a few minutes each morning has surprisingly improved my life with these little things I can see. I imagine it's improving the inside of my body in much bigger ways I cannot see.

If you're not already, I encourage you to add a breathing regimen to your morning routine. Search YouTube for some breathing exercises and find the ones you like. Also, take moments throughout the day to observe your breath. Take a slow deep breath as deeply as you can, and when you feel like you're full, take in a little more. This is how you can expand your lung capacity. When you don't use it, you lose it. Why should your lungs be any different?

After a few minutes of breathing, it's time to practice gratitude again. This time I express what I am grateful for that has *yet* to come. The trick is to feel truly grateful as if you already have it. That's what gratitude actually is. And gratitude is an emotion; how you get the things you want starts and continues with your emotions. Think of something you recently received. Maybe someone did a nice favor for you; maybe you earned a big commission payout. Maybe you got the mortgage approved for your new home. How did you feel? Happy. Excited. Grateful. This is what I call *focused manifestations*. Next, I go deeper into my focused manifestations. I guess by deeper, I mean bigger or more significant.

I focus on the bigger things I want in life, the things that are most important to me. I think about them and how I will feel when I'm doing and having them, but I conjure up the emotion of what that feels like as if I already have it. I often become moved to tears: the more tears, the deeper and more impactful the meditation.

I also do this throughout my day, conjuring up the emotion of gratitude and excitement around the goals I'm working toward or the things I want as if it's happening right then. I'm usually not consciously focusing on this practice throughout the day. The practice has just become a part of who I am and what I do. I'm in an ongoing state of excitement, an ongoing daydream. The more you practice your focused manifestations, the greater magnitude they have, and the more effortless they become.

You don't need to pressure yourself to be *good* at this practice. Just begin to make it a practice, and you will figure it out. When I first started, it was only five minutes first thing in the morning and then here and there throughout the day. I now do an hour of meditation each morning and then effortlessly here and there throughout the day. You can become a dreamer too. If you can't see it, you won't believe it. But if you can see yourself having and achieving what you want in your mind, then go deeper to begin to feel what that feels like as if you're living it right now, you will begin to believe it, and you will begin to live it.

Yoga instructors say, "Where the mind goes, the body follows." If you think you're sick or going to be sick and focus on it, you begin to feel sick. If you're excited about your presentation, you deliver it with confidence. If you're focusing on your fear of coming in second place in the interview, you inevitably mess it up. It's okay to be scared, but where is your *focus*? That's the key. Focus. Can you see yourself getting the job? Get your day and life going in the direction you want, starting with your focused manifestations. You can do these even if you're not yet sure of what you want. You know you're ready to create change. What does it *feel* like once you're there? Focus on the feeling and hold onto it, and carry this emotion throughout your day. That's manifestation. You will begin drawing toward you what you're focusing on. Good or bad, you attract what you focus on. You might as well focus on something good.

Long before I even understood what I was doing, I began this practice of conjuring up the emotion of excitement around my goals. Before I started breathwork or mediation, even before I beat my battle with anxiety and depression, this practice led me to many successes. It led me to reach my sales quotas year after year, win jobs I interviewed for, make the specific amount of money I wanted to earn each year, buy my condo, get into better shape, publish my first book, and the list will continue.

The key is in the emotion behind the thought, or the goal, the dream. And the things I've yet to master, I know I will because of how I feel. When you're thinking about something you want to improve or change in your life, think about the emotion you're feeling around it. If it's an emotion of fear or doubt, choose a different focus. Get curious about how you will feel when you do create change, get excited about it, and focus on the emotion of excitement.

Understanding Gratitude and Presence

If you listen to motivational speakers or anyone talking about the Law of Attraction and *getting present,* you've likely heard them speak on gratitude. "When you're feeling down, go into gratitude. State the things you feel grateful for." While I had been *going into gratitude for a while,* I only recently realized that I had not fully grasped the concept. The key is in your *emotions,* not in what you're saying, but in how you're feeling. If I'm saying I'm grateful but feeling sad or hurt or angry, I'm not feeling gratitude, and the practice will not be effective.

If you're tired of hearing about emotions, you might as well put this book down now because you will keep revisiting this concept throughout the pages. If you're uncomfortable exploring your emotions, that's okay. You're having a very private conversation here, even more private than just me and you. Your thoughts are between you and these pages, and I understand the personal growth process is hard. I'm rooting for you. Just as much as I believe in myself, I also believe in you.

Presence: *Existing; the ability to remain calm.*

The present is where things happen, not just things, but everything. Nowhere else can anything happen. Whatever happened in the past is no longer happening. You can sometimes make yourself feel like it is by carrying the emotion it brought on with you. By continuing to focus on your negative experiences and your feelings around them, you keep yourself reliving the experience. Remember, where you choose to focus is just that, a choice.

Consider anxiety attacks. After one attack, subsequent attacks are often brought on just by the fear of it happening again. Similarly, you can recall a painful event from the past, and the thought stimulates the same emotion you felt back then. By choosing to focus on your previously stimulated emotions, you predict your future. You will experience more of the same. You can, instead, choose to focus on this one moment you have right now. Eckhart Tolle discusses the power of a moment in his book, *The Power of Now*.

I remember the exact moment I picked up his book to read it. Although I bought the book right after someone had recommended it to me, I didn't decide to open it until several months later. I awoke one morning to the familiar stubborn cloud of depression that, at the time, I didn't know I was, in a way, responsible for. The very thing I had been trying to rid myself of my entire life, I was, in fact, creating. I had woken up to countless mornings like this. When I first opened my eyes each morning, I was present, but only for a second, before I remembered the pain. And then I would focus on the emotion of pain all day, trying to feel better, but not understanding how. You create your own realities, and while I had ups and downs, my underlying state was depressed.

But on that morning, I decided to make a different choice. Lying in bed, I remember saying to myself, almost as a plea, "Noooo. I do not want to go through my day feeling like this." My gaze wandered over to my bookshelf and settled on a book. My different choice on this day was to pick up the book and start reading. I began to learn about the power of the present moment. That was probably eight or nine years ago, and I still learn more about the present moment, even today.

Chapter 4: Becoming a Mega-Manifester

One of the first things I learned in this book was how to shift my focus from the painful thoughts inside my head to something outside myself, like a leaf. Look at its color, its texture, and how it waves in the wind. For that moment, focusing on the leaf, I felt better. Then I would remember my reasons for being sad, and again my focus was back on my sadness. But I realized that for a moment, I did feel better. Then I thought, "Okay, I'll just do it again."

This is meditation, the art of being present. Just like yoga, and just like anything, it's a practice. It's nothing to get frustrated at yourself for when you fall back into your past or drift ahead into your future. You just bring yourself back and try again. You catch yourself when your focus lapses, then consciously shift it. You can shift your attention to the people around you, listening to them, watching them. You can breathe in and breathe out. You can change your tendencies by beginning to observe them and coming back to the present moment. This moment has all the power. If you can, a few minutes of meditation is a great way to start your day. You're starting your day making a positive choice, and with one positive choice, more will follow.

What's so powerful about focusing your attention on a tree or a cloud? Remember, the present moment is the only place where something can happen. When you are present, ideas come. Do you get ideas that excite you when you're feeling angry? No. You create more anger, more frustration, more worry, more fear.

Anytime you are afraid, you are not in the present moment. And while there is a time and place to keep yourself protected, unless you're in danger, you are actually okay. You are safe. A mantra I used to tell myself when I began working on letting my guard down was: "You are safe and protected in this world." I said it over and over in my head, and it worked. Eventually, I believed it. The problem with walking around guarding myself against everyone was that I was also not open to receiving or noticing opportunities. Keeping yourself in a fear-based protective mode keeps you stuck.

Not only do you get your creative ideas and ambitions in the present moment, but you also meet people and see opportunities you would otherwise miss. I used to always walk around, inside my head and focused on what I had to get done next. Friends would later tell me they had seen me and called out my name, and I didn't hear them. I didn't turn around. So focused on achieving my tasks, I missed an opportunity to interact with someone who cared about me.

While I still write my to-do lists each week, my sense of accomplishment now comes from a different place. It comes from within. And in creating room for others in my life, would you believe I now have more time for myself? Because I'm happier, I am effortlessly more focused and get more done in less time while allowing connection with others. As humans, we seek connection. It makes sense then that you are more in harmony with yourself when you are in sync with those around you. You will go where you want faster when you live in the present moment.

The Universe often tries to get your attention to help you along your path, speaking to you through your emotions and intuition. When something feels right, it's because it is. When something feels wrong, it's because it is, at least for you. When you're in the present moment, it's easy to trust yourself and follow your intuition like a roadmap. Intuition comes before thought, before logic. I like to think of following your intuition and life direction as if you were blindfolded in the dark trying to get through a maze. You bump into a wall and meet resistance. "Don't go that way," or "There's an opening here; it feels easy and natural. Go this way."

Pay Attention to your Emotions

Your feelings are there to guide, protect, and keep you safe. How much easier is life when you pay attention to how you feel? When you go to a job you hate each day, you are ignoring the loud and clear indicator trying to get your attention that you are meant to be doing something else. When you feel great doing something or get an idea that boosts your energy, that's an indicator; that's your direction.

How do you distinguish fear from intuition? The order. Intuition comes first, guiding you in the right direction. You can feel scared when you're not in any danger. If you're not in danger and you're making a decision based on fear, the decision is going to keep you stuck. Ask yourself which emotion came first. That emotion is your direction, toward or away.

When you let fear dictate your decisions, you manifest the very thing you are trying to avoid because you let fear stop you from trying. Then, of course, you won't get the job. Of course, you won't close the deal. Of course, the relationship will end. Remember to pay attention to the first emotion you felt when you came up with your new idea. If the emotion is excitement, and fear kicks in after, go back to the emotion of excitement. Observe the fear, push it aside, and choose to lead with the excitement. Whichever emotion you choose to focus on is your choice. Taking responsibility for yourself in these moments is empowering. And once you do it enough times, you'll have a new habit, a new state of mind, and a roadmap to success.

If staying present is new to you, it will be challenging, and that's okay. Remember to observe and catch yourself. When you fall off track, redirect yourself. One encouraging side effect of this practice is that after a while, although your attention might drift back on occasion to the not-so-fun neighborhood of your past, you will notice that your emotions are now different when the memory surfaces. Maybe it doesn't hurt that much anymore, maybe not even at all. While the memory is still there, the once unpleasant emotion associated with it is now lighter. This is because you are in the present moment. If you burned your hand on the stove and later recalled this event, the memory is there, but the pain is not.

Your emotions are important because you attract more of how you are feeling. So even though you remember things that once felt bad, it's important to remember they're not happening to you now. The present moment is where all things happen, and *only* where things happen. It is in the present moment you have the power to create. It is here that you can learn to create the life you want.

Turn your Frustration into Focus

Your frustration can go undetected for a long time before it gets big enough for you to take notice. Sometimes, by the time your frustration becomes too big to stop ignoring, you look back and realize you've been unhappy for a long time. Usually, thinking back, you can spot the first moment when your frustration showed up. Maybe your energy sank. Maybe you got one of those *bad* butterflies. I distinguish bad butterflies from nervous butterflies as it can be good to be nervous. Nervousness can be a byproduct of excitement. You have some stake in the game. When you're paying attention, your frustration can be the spark that gets your attention, then the flame that fuels your fire. When you're paying attention, frustration can easily transform into momentum—another way presence can carry you further down your path faster. Vroom.

Frustration serves a purpose. It's pointing you in a new direction. When the box no longer fits, it's time to step outside of it. Of course, the new box you step into is also uncomfortable because it's different, but you have to move. You work to find comfort when you're uncomfortable, which requires growth. Therefore, discomfort is a tool. Anytime you get a twinge of *"Ugh, I don't like this,"* it's time to move; time to take action. These subtle, or sometimes not so subtle, hints, depending on how long you've been ignoring them, are your intuition. You often stick with what's familiar until your discomfort has grown big enough for you to take a chance and venture out into the unknown. It's human nature to want to predict your future. When you know what to expect, you feel safe. But when you choose predictability, you limit yourself.

Forget the How – Just Move

As you begin acknowledging and pursuing the life you want, remember that *how it's going to work* is not important. *How* is not even your business. When I'm setting out to achieve a goal, I have no idea exactly how I'll do it. I fully trust I will figure it out as I go. If I knew exactly how all the steps would be laid out, I would easily miss the great new ideas that emerge along the way. I have come to realize another meaning behind the phrase *The joy is in the ride and not the destination*; it's not just for your experiences, but for the new ideas that surface and the people you meet along the way. It's your business only to know where you're heading and get started.

When setting out to achieve a goal, your work is to feel the emotion of how you will feel once you achieve what you're setting out to. Let this emotion of excitement fuel the momentum that carries you to steps two, three, and four. Each step will come when you're ready, and you will see it when you're present. Focus on the emotion of excitement, and the first step will appear. Your work is to allow yourself to dream, letting your creative ideas surface. Then practice gratitude, as if you already have what it is you're aiming for. Your work is to know with certainty that the things calling you are meant for you. Yes, you can, of course, you can. No need to look for even the first step. It will show up.

Anyone can change direction at any time in their life by employing these practices that are so simple children can, and do, do them. The process of daydreaming and manifesting comes naturally to kids, which means it once came naturally to you.

Chapter 4 Exercise: Identify and Remember Achievements

Before moving on to the next chapter, think back to something you achieved as a kid. It could be making the baseball team, winning the art contest, or getting the lead in the school play. Take a moment to try and take yourself back there. Play the memory back in your mind and try and remember how you felt. Did you envision yourself doing what you were aiming to do before you actually did it? You do this as an adult, too, every day and all day with all the things you need to get done. Before beginning the task, effortlessly, in your mind's eye, you see yourself completing it.

Master your Mindset

1. Begin each day with a few minutes of your favorite deep breathing exercises.

2. Add the practice of gratitude to your morning routine by feeling the emotion as if you already have the things you want.

3. Carry the emotion of excitement with you throughout your day as you think about your goals.

4. Observe your thoughts and emotions. When they drift to an uncomfortable memory of the past or you find yourself worried about the uncertainty of the future, take a deep breath, let the emotion pass, and choose to focus back on the excitement of where you're heading.

Some Extra Encouragement ...

Before you unload the dishwasher, in your mind's eye, you first see yourself doing it. Before you make the bed, a vision of yourself smoothing out the comforter flashes through your head. Now you're just learning how to apply the same concept to the bigger, more meaningful things you want. And whatever you want or dream of is for a reason.

This chapter discussed mindset, focus, presence, meditation, and how to manifest. If you're feeling like you're not sure what you're getting yourself into, we will simplify it in the next chapter. Let's go back to where all things start: the beginning.

Chapter Five

Innocence Is Power

Chapter 5: Innocence Is Power

Inexperience Allows the Element of Surprise

"Children are not things to be molded, but are people to be unfolded."
~*Jess Lair, Author*

Innocence: *Pure; lacking experience; harmless.*

If knowledge is power, then the power in innocence is the element of surprise. Not knowing allows you to be excited, to be present. Learning from your experiences can sometimes hinder you to the same degree it can help. When you hold onto negative emotions, you keep yourself stuck. Your perspective forms your mindset, which influences your decisions, which then creates your life. You can learn to view the unknown as a gift, something to get excited about. Where you choose to focus your mind is where you will go. Get excited.

Taking a Lesson from Kids

It's a good thing kids are naïve. Otherwise, how would they ever learn to walk? Kids' naivety is what helps them to be fearless. While I am fearless in pursuing my dreams, there are a couple of things I am afraid of—as I shared earlier, just two. One is going to the doctor, and the other is falling down—literally falling down. I'm not afraid to try and risk failing because I know I won't. I might learn that an endeavor I began to pursue doesn't feel right, and then I'll shift my focus. But if the direction feels right, there will be no failure. I will keep going no matter how many times I fall. Literally falling down is another story. This scares me; I imagine it stems from a need to control, to keep myself emotionally safe. While I have come a long way in my journey, some elements of my former self still linger.

Literally Falling Down

I learned to ride a bike later than most. While the other neighborhood kids seemed to embrace the idea with fearless excitement, I was petrified—so petrified that until I was seven years old, I rode in the baby seat on the back of my stepmother's bike. My dad, stepmom, older sister, and two older stepbrothers rode their own bikes on family bike rides while my seven-year-old too-long-for-a-baby-seat legs dangled from the back of my stepmom's bike.

I would have been content to remain in the baby seat until I was old enough to just stay home by myself. But when my little sister, an actual baby, was big enough to come along for the bike rides, I got bumped from the baby seat. It was time for me to learn.

I remember my first bike. It was a used bike, probably from a neighborhood garage sale, pastel pink with a white banana seat. While I was terrified to ride it, I loved the bike. My dad would hold the back of the seat while I pedaled, and I remember the first time I actually kept going after he let go. Looking back at him, this time, my legs kept going. This time my emotion of excitement was greater than the one of fear. I was suddenly pedaling down the street all on my own. I rode around our cul-de-sac and then flew

Chapter 5: Innocence Is Power

down the little hill on our street, my long hair flying. I was comfortable with the familiar terrain of our perfectly paved street and rode my bike with confidence. No surprises. I had graduated to riding my own bike.

One sunny weekend afternoon, the family ventured out of the safety of our little neighborhood for a bike ride at the city park. I sat in the back of our station wagon between my stepbrothers, butterflies swarming my stomach as we approached our destination. As I watched my parents unload our bikes, my terror grew. I longed to ride in the baby seat. With much trepidation, I climbed onto my pink bike and began the trek. A little ways into the bike ride, the moment came, the moment I dreaded—uneven terrain. I had to cross a little bridge over a stream of water, and once I passed it, I would then have to maneuver my bike around a giant tree surrounded by a patch of prickly bushes.

Cowering in fear, I lingered behind. I remember my family stopped and waited for me on the other side. They were cheering me on to come over the little bridge. In my seven-year-old mind, it was a bridge. But remembering back, it was a wide stretch of sidewalk with plenty of room on either side, serving as the pass over a little stream of water. I would have had to steer my bike directly toward the water to fall into it, but still, I was panicked. Having no choice, eventually, I mustered up the confidence and pedaled over the bridge.

Next, I had to tackle the big corner turn to avoid crashing into the tree. I was scared to turn my bike. If I didn't turn my handlebars, guiding my pink banana seat bike around the bend, I would instead drive straight into the giant tree and fall over into the patch of bushes. After I'd safely conquered the so-called bridge, I kept going, not slowing down as I approached the tree. "Turn Amy, turn!" my family called out, their voices muffled against the audible thud of my pounding heartbeats. In slow motion, I played the scene out in my head, the one where I ran straight into the tree and fell over, scratching up my legs on the bushes. I was apparently more scared of turning my bike than falling because I drove straight into the tree and fell right into the bushes. That's my story about learning to ride a bike.

I eventually learned how to turn my bike without fear, but I do not ride a bike these days. I still don't like anything that involves the possibility of literally falling down. You won't catch me ice-skating, skiing, or hopping on one of the readily available Citibikes all over Manhattan. I like my feet planted firmly on the ground while keeping my head forever in the clouds. It works for me. I'm even scared when bike riders appear to be pedaling right toward me at a fast pace. While they are likely paying attention, I don't have control over what they're doing, so I'm always a bit uncomfortable when there are a bunch of cyclists around.

Most kids are fearless when approaching a new experience. Their excitement is stronger than their fear, and this momentum pushes them to take the first step. Why do most adults not succeed in getting what they want? I would wager it's because they haven't tried. What if you could unlearn what your bad experiences have taught you? You can, by focusing on a different emotion.

Get Back to Being a Kid

In many ways, you can take a lesson from kids by asking their favorite question: "Why?" Kids are not afraid to ask why. They're not yet afraid to ask, "What if?" Little kids daydream off to fantasy land, and no dream is too big. They're going to be movie stars or astronauts. It's not until you get older and endure some negative experiences that you learn about fear and let it begin to influence your decisions. What if you allowed yourself to become childlike again? When you don't understand something for fear of the unknown, you can go further by getting curious about it instead of avoiding it. Instead of sticking with what you know when you already know it doesn't feel that great, you can discover something different when you allow yourself to get curious about a different path. Change happens when you allow yourself to wonder, "What might that be like?"

What if, before making a decision, you asked yourself, what would a little kid do? You might get much closer to your real self, to the parts of yourself you haven't let out to play for a while. Kids are not afraid to be themselves. They're not afraid to get up and try again when they fall. They're not afraid to speak their mind. They're not afraid to admit they want something and to go for it. The thing that holds us back is fear. Doesn't it make sense, then, that if you choose the opposite of fear, you are guaranteed to be more successful?

I know a guy, a funny guy. His dream is to be a standup comedian; each week, he goes to open mics to practice his craft. He writes, working on his material, and he makes people laugh. He even lights up the room, his energy effortlessly commanding attention. The crowd loves him. They want more.

A little kid would keep going, building upon this energy, choosing to take risks and dream big. A little kid would ask himself, "What if?"

What if it works out?

What if I get passed at this comedy club and the next comedy club?

What if I get a tour?

What if I get a spot on late-night TV?

A little kid would get curious. His curiosity would lead to excitement, which would build momentum, influencing his positive choices and his persistent belief in himself that he can and will achieve his dream.

The life you create for yourself is a product of the choices you make each day. You do have control over your choices, and you do have control over your mindset. Therefore, you have control over your life. The circumstances you find yourself in as an adult, you created. Taking responsibility for yourself can be scary because the only blame you can then place is on yourself. But your success or failure is ultimately up to you. This awareness can be more empowering than scary when you understand that you can create the life you want.

The funny guy made some mistakes in his past. He considered himself lucky to get the job he did when he was 22 years old. The funny guy is now in his 50s, working the exact same job he got at 22. What happened? Did he ask himself, "What if there's more? A promotion? A different job altogether? What if I can?" Did he let himself wonder, get excited, then let his emotions lead to actions that created success? Or did he choose the perspective of "What if I can't?" and let this mindset keep him stuck?

How you do anything is how you do everything. This funny guy chose not to try that hard in his career or his comedy. He chose to do the bare minimum to get by, ignoring that little voice inside of him that wants more, that knows there is more. His mindset dictates his choices which create his life—a life of lack.

It's never too late to switch your mindset at any time or at any age. Start with "I wonder," just like a kid, and see where that takes you. Play make-believe. Let yourself not only imagine, but feel the dream that you want as if it's actually happening right now. Enjoy the feeling, touch it each day and carry it with you. Your dominant emotions do influence your choices, which then create either setbacks or opportunities. Something else my grandfather told me is, "You're in control." And so are you.

Seeing Is Succeeding

Kids love to play the game of *make-believe*. And when they're in it, they're really in it. Kids are actually doing focused manifestations and manifesting what they focus on all day long. They see themselves riding a bike, and they learn how. They look at the monkey bars, the vision of crossing them flashes through their little minds, and off they go. Not me, by the way. I was not most kids. I never tackled the monkey bars because I was afraid of falling. But I watched as other kids swung across them like, well, brave little monkeys. Belief in yourself is actually innate. Perhaps it's just time for a reminder.

Who would have thought that daydreaming could be the key to success? When you allow yourself to feel your dreams as if you are currently living them, you feel like they're happening. Your brain thinks your goals are happening, and your body naturally starts on the path that takes you where you want to go. Carry yourself forward with your thoughts, and let your body follow your excited emotions.

You can also learn a lot from kids' favorite question: "Why?" How can this innocent question help you go further? It's curiosity. When you adopt the attitude of wonder, you open yourself to possibilities. Conversely, when you choose worry, and it is a choice, you keep yourself stuck.

How many times have you heard mothers say, "I'm a mom; it's my job to worry"? Likely many times. I would typically challenge my mother on this, arguing, "What good does worrying do?" to which she would challenge me back. Once, she said, "Don't you worry about your little cousin?" My little cousin, who is fine? Do I just conjure up some worry for her? No, I don't do this. This would be creating negative energy for her and around her and sending it her way. If there is someone who is actually sick or who needs help, worrying for them would still not be my practice. Instead, I would conjure up healing, happy, healthy emotions around them and for them, thinking and feeling positively, envisioning them healthy and feeling better, and send this state of mind their way energetically. I actually do this as part of my morning meditation each day.

Kids are not afraid to dream. Kids are not afraid to ask *why*. Kids are not afraid to fall, and kids are not afraid to try and keep trying. Kids are not afraid to show their excitement about what they're pursuing. Kids are not afraid … until they learn *how to be*. Your experiences teach you to be scared. You want to protect yourself. But what if you could *unteach* yourself? What if you could learn how to be like a kid again, just by letting yourself get excited?

Fear Is Limiting – Excitement Is Limitless

What if the key to success is in your emotions? Think of someone you know who succeeded at something, a business venture, a career change, or a personal goal. Try and remember back to when they first got started. What was their attitude around their idea? Maybe they had a glimmer of doubt. But unless they told you about it, you didn't know because their fear was not their focus. Their focus was on their excitement.

The excitement around their idea helps successful people propel themselves forward with confidence in their pursuit. First, they get excited, and then they get started. Their mindset is the foundation of their success. By remaining present and excited with their vision at the forefront of their mind, they see their first step when it shows up and then the next. And each step they take further instills their confidence, propelling them forward. Successful people listen to their emotions and trust their intuition. The key to success is mindset. The same is true with failure. The indicator of how things will work out, good or bad, is your mindset, or attitude, because your attitude dictates your choices that create your reality.

You may get ideas. But whether you listen to your ideas, trust your instincts, and follow your excitement, is a choice. A successful person's attitude is no different than a kid's before they later learn that life can disappoint them. Life's challenges become much easier to navigate when you listen to and honor what feels right. Life is as hard as you make it for yourself.

Successful, and I should add, happy people stay in the present moment. When fear or doubt creep in, they just bring themselves right back, observing the negative thought, then releasing it as quickly as it came. This is a practice that *takes practice*, and without judgment. You don't need to be perfect at it to succeed and improve your life. You just try and keep trying, and eventually, you do change. Things can only happen in the present moment. Staying in it as much as possible is key.

Curiosity vs. Separation

While it is human nature to seek connection with your community, it also seems to be human nature to gravitate toward what you can understand. Fear of what you don't understand leads to separation, and when you're in separation, you're in disharmony. When you keep yourself at a distance from people who are different or keep yourself from exploring experiences of which you don't know the outcome, you create a reality of isolation and a feeling of disconnect.

When you encounter these types of situations and emotions, you have choices. You can approach the situation as an opportunity to get curious and learn more about yourself and each other. You can approach new experiences, good or bad, with the innocence and curiosity of a kid. When you get and stay curious, you uncover, discover, and ultimately, you grow.

As you lose your innocence, learning from your experiences, you can become resistant. Separating or protecting yourself from the people or things you are unfamiliar with is avoiding connection. And when you avoid connection, you miss opportunities. You also feel empty. When you choose to embrace the unknown, the possibilities are also unknown. They are limitless. When you limit yourself to what you know, you are limited.

Fear of the *Unknown* or Fear of the *Known?*

If you're someone who doesn't like venturing out into the unknown, you may be keeping yourself stuck in certain areas of your life. What question most influences your mindset when you think about the things you want? Is it "What if it doesn't work out?" Or is it "What if it *does* work out?" You attract more of how you're feeling, and how you're feeling influences your decisions. If you're feeling doubtful, your doubt will guide you. If your dominant emotion around your idea is excitement, that excitement predicts your future. Where your mind goes, you will follow.

An Unrealistic True Story

When I was close to graduating college, I was feeling adventurous. I decided I wanted to pick a city I'd never been to, where I knew no one, and move there. Although ultimately I knew I belonged in New York, I chose Seattle for my post-graduation adventure, taking me the furthest I could get from New York. I don't claim to have been a logical young woman in my twenties. I actually dropped out of my Logic class. Logic counted toward my math requirement, and I thought it sounded easier than Geometry. Turns out, for me, it was not. Sensible or not, when I set my mind to something, I'm doing it. Thankfully I've learned to be more discerning in choosing my direction. But back then, I still had quite a ways to go.

My apartment lease in Kansas City was up, and as my next move was still uncertain, my dad suggested I move back in with him, and so I did. My sights set on Seattle, I found myself in an unexpected relationship and then struggled with whether to stay or go. I waivered back and forth until one morning, I made my decision. Seattle, here I come. While my dad was away at work, I packed up my car and my cat, Lacy. I grabbed a spoon and a jar of peanut butter for some fuel during my trip, left my poor dad a note on the kitchen counter, and started on the thirty-hour drive to Seattle, Washington.

Stuck in traffic while departing the city, again, I began to question my decision. My hastily crammed belongings felt as though they were caving in around me. I pushed on, and many hours later, I found myself driving through the serene atmosphere of Montana and then Idaho. The air was clean and fresh, bringing with it a sense of freedom. The myriad of bikers on their Harley Davidsons heading to Sturgis brought a sense of safety. Cruising down the highway with my music playing, I felt excited about what lay ahead. I felt like singing and dancing, and then, out of nowhere, came another irrational idea, even more irrational than my move across the country.

I decided I was going to become a dancer. I had no formal training, not since tap dance class when I was probably five. Still, the more I thought about becoming a dancer, the more excited I got.

One night during my three-day trip, I stopped at a gas station to fill up. It was around midnight. My cat managed to escape from the car as I didn't have her in a carrier. As I said, logic was not my thing back then. I found myself chasing Lacy around the gas station in the middle of nowhere. Somehow, I eventually got her safely back into the car. I remember driving down the highway through the night with her even crawling onto the top of my head at one point. By some miracle, I arrived in Seattle.

Chapter 5: Innocence Is Power

I remember being surprised at how hilly the city was. I drove through town and past the Mariner's stadium. It was beautiful. I arrived at my apartment downtown and went into the office. The apartment manager gave me the key and told me to park my car on the sidewalk, which was on a very steep hill, and unload my belongings. I did, and Lacy and I were home for the next three and half weeks until I freaked out and had an anxiety attack, realizing how far away I was from everyone and everything I knew. Afterward, I moved my belongings and my cat back into my car and drove back to Kansas City to move back in with my dad. Pause for laughter.

But here's what happened during the short time I was there. If you recall the drama television series *Melrose Place*, that's kind of what my apartment building was like. The apartments surrounded a courtyard like a horseshoe, opening to an inground pool. The Capri Apartments are still there. I did a Google search recently and took a trip down memory lane. Lots of other young people were living there at the time, and we'd all hang around the pool talking in the evenings. Sometimes we'd walk down to Vito's, this little restaurant that had karaoke. It was dark and cozy with red leather booths. I had fun. I sang songs and made friends easily.

I even made a good friend the same day I moved in. I found the people in Seattle open, friendly, and receptive to me. They smiled at me on the streets, and I seemed to fit in well, much better than I had in the Midwest. While I did have some good friends in Kansas City, I never truly fit in there. My direct nature seemed abrasive to the locals, and their "politeness" to me didn't feel genuine. But Seattle somehow was just as I thought it would be. I liked it. I arrived on a summer day in June, and having only stayed just shy of a month, I never did experience the rainy, dreary season. I have always liked the rain, though.

I guess I didn't even have a cell phone then. I had a used computer my dad had gotten me, and I had to wait for my dial-up internet service to be installed. With my cat and my belongings safely inside my temporary new home, I decided it was time to go to the store. I needed some things. But where was the store? With no phone and no internet, how would I find it? I walked outside and just stood there for a moment, looking around. A guy walking by stopped and looked at me with a big smile on his face. "You look like you need help," he said.

"I do," I said. "Do you know where Target is?" His name, fittingly, was Smiley, and we became friends. Smiley told me how to get to Target. He even took me out and showed me around Seattle. He was a talented freestyle rapper, and people knew him wherever we went. One night we went out, and he got up on stage at this club and did his thing. Everyone loved him. We walked past some tall grungy looking guys with long straggly hair. Smiley said, "Do you know who that was?" I didn't. We had just passed a member of Alice in Chains. I don't remember which one. But they were nice and said "hello" to Smiley.

When I was alone in my apartment, I danced. I let myself get more and more excited about becoming a dancer. No logic. No idea how. I just knew it was going to happen. I felt it. I was excited.

I loved exploring the city. I applied at some restaurants hoping to find a serving job first, and then eventually, I'd figure out my career direction. I went to Pike's Place Market and watched the fish mongers throwing and catching fish. I went to the open-air coffee shops. I loved the coffee shops. The first one I went to, I remember being surprised when a friendly stranger sat down at my table. "Hello," he said and then went to reading his paper and sipping his coffee. Strangers didn't share tables in Kansas City. But in Seattle, if the tables were all taken and you had an empty chair at yours, someone was going to take the seat. I found it refreshing.

One day, while walking around exploring, I went into another coffee shop. On my way to the bathroom, I stopped to check out their community bulletin board and noticed an advertisement for a traveling dance team. I stopped to read it. The opportunity didn't require any previous dance experience. They would interview you, and if they liked you and felt you'd be a good fit for their team, you could join. They covered room and board and would teach you how to dance.

Previous members had gone on to have careers in dance, either joining other professional dance teams or opening their own studios. I took the information and decided to apply. They interviewed me and … drum roll … I got it. They liked me for their team. I couldn't believe it, except I could. I had manifested this completely irrational opportunity through sheer excitement. I got the idea, got excited, and then I just led with the emotion of excitement. This is how manifestation works. There was no rationality, and there was also no worry. There was just my idea and my positive emotion.

They were genuinely disappointed when I decided to turn the opportunity down. While my actions around my trip to Seattle and my decision to move there were not exactly responsible choices, I did decide that I had a responsibility to my cat. I couldn't drag the poor baby across the country and then give her away to move in and travel with the dance team. But it's pretty special and miraculous that I could have made my then dream of becoming a dancer come true with nothing other than my thoughts.

Knowing and Not Knowing Is Succeeding

Successful people know one thing. They know they will succeed. There is also something they don't know. They don't yet know what the journey will look like, which means they don't know *how*. That's where the beauty is, in the not knowing. They let themselves get excited and then choose to lead with the emotion of excitement. This keeps them present so that when the first step shows up, they can easily see it and trust their direction.

You also have the power to become superhuman. Isn't it superhuman to create something just from an idea? But then that's where all creation stems from. You have ideas. The difference for people whose ideas become their reality is the way they think. They believe in themselves.

When you are curious and excited, seeing and feeling the limitless possibilities in your mind, you become magnetic, drawing opportunities toward you. You don't have to do anything. I got the idea that I wanted to become a dancer. Not only did I want to, but *I was going* to. I didn't do a thing other than get excited. I didn't research any dance studios. I didn't take one class. Yet, there it was, the opportunity staring back at me when I happened to walk into that particular coffee shop and stopped to look at the bulletin board.

Change Your Perspective, Change Your Life

While being easy on yourself, observe your mindset. When you find yourself thinking the familiar thought, *"What if it doesn't work out?"* switch it: *"What if it does?"* And then take it further with curiosity and excitement. Get feeling good about the things that you want because they are coming. Conjure up the feeling as if they are happening right now at this moment. Feel how that feels and let this excitement carry you forward, influencing your decisions. Likely, if you look back throughout your life and the things you've achieved, you did exactly this. You got an idea, envisioned yourself doing whatever it was, got excited, told yourself you could, and then you got started.

The things that didn't work out or have yet to work out for you, and for me, you likely carry the emotion of fear around your idea, goal, or desire. You do predict your future. And if you must know what yours looks like before taking that step, take a moment to observe your emotions. How do you feel about certain areas of your life? You will continue to succeed in the areas in which you feel good.

In the areas you don't feel so good, maybe it's time to switch things up. Instead of fearing it won't work out, get excited as if you're living out what you want right now. You are now predicting your new future. It takes practice, retraining your brain. Changing a negative mindset is like changing a bad habit. It's not easy, but it also doesn't have to be nearly as hard as you think.

If there's something you want to change, envision the changes and then get excited as if it's already happening. You do this all the time without even noticing. You're either nervous or excited when standing in line for a roller coaster ride as if you're already on the ride. Your brain thinks you are, so your body starts acting like you are. Maybe you have butterflies flying around your stomach; maybe your heart is beating faster.

I get very nervous about going to the doctor because I've fainted there so many times before, and I have unnecessarily re-created this bad experience for myself many times. I start getting nervous on the way to my physical, and my pulse begins dropping even though I'm not yet anywhere near the needle that I know will be going into my arm. By the time I arrive, the nurse can't take my blood because my pulse is too low, and with each attempt of her trying to stick me, my pulse drops more; I become weaker and feel faint.

Now when I go to get my blood drawn, I do my best to make sure I'm feeling really good that day. When I'm in good spirits, the appointment goes just fine.

While I have plenty of examples proving my manifestations, I'm the same as everyone else. My mindset, good or bad, predicts my future. It's natural for glimmers of doubt to creep in. Your work moving forward is to trust yourself, your ideas, and that they are coming to you for a reason. Then let the emotion of excitement be your leading emotion. Observe and acknowledge the fear when it surfaces, and choose to put your focus on the emotion of excitement. Lead with excitement.

Let's Get Honest

One special gift kids have is actually something they lack—the ability to sugarcoat things. Kids don't know what that is; they just say what they think. As adults, you often don't say what you actually think for fear you may not be well-received or that you may offend. The problem with this is that you can only learn from each other when you're being honest with one another. You can only be close to others when you are being honest. Without honesty, there is no intimacy. Without vulnerability, there is no connection.

Kids aren't afraid to say how they feel or show how they feel. The tendency to hold back as an adult can keep you disconnected, creating lack in your life. The instinct to trust and express yourself is innate. You can live a richer life when you get past your fear by choosing to awaken these inherent qualities that have perhaps been dormant in certain areas of your life. The truth is, if you're not being honest with others, then you're not being honest with yourself, which means you are not *being* yourself. And when you're not being yourself, you attract people and things that don't align with you.

Start paying attention to how you feel around certain company and work to be brave enough to let go of people and situations that don't feel authentic to you. When you're feeling misunderstood by others, the best thing to do is get to know yourself better. Spend time hanging out with yourself. Time alone takes the pressure off to portray happiness when you're not feeling it. It gives you space and time to discover yourself more deeply. And it creates room for the right people to come into your life. In doing this myself, my confidence grew. I learned to accept myself, and this was when friends I felt aligned with began to come into my life. But I still had some work to do.

Still Seeking Acceptance outside of Myself

While I had grown to feel much happier and more fulfilled, I observed that I felt my confidence sink each time I went home to visit. I didn't understand why other people in my life appreciated me, valuing my insights, while my family always seemed to dismiss me. Each time I attempted to contribute to the conversation I'd just traveled eight hours to be a part of, the subject would get changed, and everyone's attention redirected. Or I'd get disapproving eyes rolled at me. Each time I returned to New York from a family visit, it would take days to lift my spirits again.

One thing I always enjoyed doing when visiting my mom and stepdad was going grocery shopping and cooking a nice dinner. Once while making dinner, I donned an oven mitt and reached into the oven. These oven mitts were bright red and made of rubber. Whoever's bright idea it was to make rubber oven mitts didn't consider how hard it actually is to grip anything while wearing them. As I was pulling the tray out of the oven, I lost my grip, and my forearm bumped the top rung, burning my arm.

I didn't make a big deal out of it, especially because my mother sighed like she had so many times before, as if I were *a problem*. And my stepfather rolled his eyes and walked out of the kitchen. I made a joke, "There goes my hand modeling career!" and just kept preparing dinner. I didn't even stop to tend to my burn, and as a result, it scarred, a forever reminder of that moment. My feelings were hurt. I had become a well-adjusted, responsible and successful adult, yet I still found myself feeling like a problem back in my parent's kitchen. Making the long drive to see them and doing something nice for them didn't mean anything. In their eyes, I was still difficult. I was still a problem.

Chapter 5: Innocence Is Power

Despite all the work I had done to feel better, deep down, I still didn't. Their perception of me still affected my perception of myself. I wanted to feel better. I kept trying to solve the problem by observing it more closely in an effort to understand *why* it was happening. I even tried talking to my family about it, which only resulted in arguments erupting and my family not talking to me. Trying to get them to understand me instead of trying to understand myself better only led to more pain. Finally, one day I figured it out.

When someone is acting irrational, you don't want to upset them further. It's easier just to follow their lead, even when it doesn't feel right, than it is to speak up and rock the boat. I was the boat rocker in my family and had become the outcast from a very young age. I only recently came to understand that when others don't set healthy boundaries for themselves, they are likely resistant to those who do. My self-empowerment, when I tried to just *be* myself by contributing to the conversation or standing up for myself when I wasn't being treated well, was making my family feel disempowered.

When people try to bring others down in an effort to make themselves feel better, they end up feeling worse and not understanding why.

After I figured out what was going on with my family and concluded that I would not be able to *get them to see me* and understand me, I succumbed to the fact that I was just going to have to not need them. And for two years, I did not speak to them, and I was mostly okay with it. It takes practice to let the hurt and anger go. But when you can step outside of yourself and become an observer of yourself, you can change your reactions, and that is where the change happens, in your reactions.

If something in your life keeps coming up that you don't like and feel you don't have control over, consider what you *do* have control over. You can control your reaction, and you can choose a different one. When you do, the result will surely be different. This is how you break deep-rooted patterns that are keeping you stuck.

The two years without speaking to my family had gone by when I learned my stepfather had become very sick. I only found out from my dad. My sister told him, and he told me. I drove home a couple of days later and showed up at the hospital. Of course, I was nervous I might not be received, but showing up was what I needed to do.

A couple of days later, I was sitting in the hospital lobby with my mother, brother, and sister. And I "observed" that *the thing* was happening again. Each time I tried to join in the conversation, my mother would dismiss me, not look at me, ignore me, change the subject, and instead focus all of her attention on my brother or my sister. It wasn't enough that I had worked so hard on myself all these years to continue bettering myself. It wasn't enough that I rented a car, drove eight hours, and showed up to be there with a positive and supportive attitude. It was still not enough. My mother was showing me that I was still not enough. I was still "the problem."

But then I identified the real problem. The problem that had been holding me back in one very important area of my life was that I was adopting my mother's opinion of me. The problem was not that she thought I wasn't enough. The problem was my perception of myself. Enter another defining moment. Here I was reliving the same experience yet in different surroundings. But on this day, I would change my reaction.

First, I observed what was happening; my brother and sister were just going along with my mother when it was clear what she was doing. Second, I observed not only what my mother was doing, but I also observed myself slipping back into my old pattern of giving up and getting quiet after my third attempt at joining the conversation: "Do not cast pearls before swine." If someone's not listening, I stop talking.

But the same problem kept showing up for me, not only here with my family, but in other areas of my life as well. And it would keep showing up until I changed my response to the problem. My act of observing and then shifting my perspective all happened within seconds, and I knew this was my moment. It was time for me to push past this problem so that it would finally stop defining me, so that I could begin living the life I wanted, one where I felt understood and accepted.

I didn't realize until then that the person I needed acceptance from was myself. While I will never forget any of my experiences, the moment had come for me to shift my perspective and create a new future in this area of my life. While as a kid, I was scared of falling down, I was never afraid of standing up for myself. It was time for me to become that fearless little kid again who once stood up for herself, even to her family, no matter the consequences.

This moment changed things. The painful emotions I'd bottled and carried with me since I was a little girl, which came out to play in full force when I was around my family, once again had every nerve in my body on end. I wanted to storm out of the hospital, get into my rental car and drive the eight hours back to New York that instant. But I wasn't going to do that while my stepfather lay dying on the fourth floor. I sat at the table in the hospital lobby with my mother, brother, and sister, and while I was once again feeling angry, hurt, and ignored, it was time for me to change my reaction.

"I have something to say."

I spoke up. I told my mother what she was doing and what she had done all these years, and she, again, did what she always had done. She immediately started to cry and blamed me. My sister interrupted, trying to keep me from saying what I needed to say in an effort to appease my mother. I didn't stop. I told her what she had done and what they all had done.

"That is why I walked away from this family," I said. And next, I said the most important words of all. Although I said them out loud, they were for me more than anyone else. Firmly, I said, "I–have–value," and then I got up and walked away. This is the change that was needed, the change in my reaction to the same bad experience that kept showing up. The surface-level problem was my family ignoring me. The same problem surfaced in other areas of my life as well, leaving me feeling the same emotions—hurt, ignored, abandoned, and unaccepted.

All along, the answer I was searching for was within myself. It was not getting my mother to see my value, to apologize, or feel remorse for how she treated me all these years and for how she was still treating me. If that were the solution, then the problem would never be solved because she still hasn't taken responsibility for her actions. In taking responsibility for myself, for my feelings about myself, I saw value in myself. And that was what I needed, self-acceptance.

If I see my value and feel value and acceptance from myself, I don't need to look for it, not in any relationship. So once I uncovered and resolved the real issue within myself, which was that I needed to value myself, then the surface-level symptomatic problems of the real issue began to go away. Just like when your cold clears up, so does your runny nose; when the real issue, the real illness, goes away, so do your surface-level problems.

My relationship with my mother has not changed. But how I see myself has, and as a result, the pain is much less. Many days I don't feel it at all. Other days it comes back to visit, and I deal with it by acknowledging it and giving myself the love I need. We'll talk more about how to do this later.

When you change your reactions to the problems that keep showing up, you get different results. You get *the unknown*, versus more of *the known*.

If you find yourself struggling to stand up for yourself in certain areas of your life or choosing to remain around company that doesn't value you, ask yourself what your younger self would do. That little kid who was still naïve to consequences, what would he do? What would she do? Kids often have it figured out, following their nature, their instincts, before they learn to develop logic and fear. You can be more like a kid again. It's still your nature.

Yes, I was scared to stand up for myself with my family as an adult. I was scared to again be the boat rocker. But I was more scared to go on living a life of dis-ease inside myself. The decision to become that fearless kid again changed my life. It reshaped my outlook and my state of mind. Every day I wake up on fire with so much love for myself, so much gratitude for what I have and for what I know is coming. At that moment, by deciding to change my reaction, I changed my future.

My hope is that after reading this chapter, you feel some weight lifted and that the pressure of creating change now feels a bit easier. When you get back to your nature and become the fearless younger version of yourself, now equipped with years of experience and knowledge on how to better care for yourself, that's powerful. Let this power fuel your momentum as you work to improve yourself each day, and as you turn the page to the next chapter and the next phase of your life. But first, this chapter exercise should help lock in the message.

Chapter 5 Exercise: Reparenting

Now that you're warmed up and well on your way to becoming a better version of yourself with each day, it's time to do the Reparenting exercise. This one might be tougher, but you're here to do some inner work, and you're now about halfway through the book. You're ready. This exercise can teach you a way to cease looking outside of yourself for the answers by teaching you to give yourself what it is you're searching for. This is a form of reparenting. I have done it myself, and I find it very effective; I do it now and again as needed when some old familiar pain comes up. Here goes. You can do this.

Start by sitting in a quiet space, alone and with your eyes closed. Begin to take some deep breaths and focus on your breathing. Next is the hard part. Think of something that hurts you. Consider how this emotion keeps you feeling stuck in a certain area of your life. Can you identify the real underlying issue that is holding you back? Can you trace this feeling of discontent back to a painful past event? Go deeper. Can you remember back to an earlier experience when you first felt this emotion?

It will likely take some digging to get there, as most of us have blocked out our most painful memory. I had as well. It doesn't necessarily have to be about your parents. It can be a different experience involving someone else that had a traumatic effect on you. Start with whatever most painful and furthest back memory you can think of. Likely, the deeper one will eventually surface. Whichever memory you can remember back to, try and remember the emotion you felt.

Watch the experience in your mind as if you are watching a movie. Picture your younger self reliving the event. Watch the scene. It will be painful. That's okay. You will feel the same pain you felt back then. Let it come up. Let yourself feel it. Let yourself cry and feel sad. Give the emotion the experience brings up a label. "Unloved." "Unaccepted." "Abandoned." Whatever the feeling, sit with it for a moment longer.

Now walk into the scene; you, as your older self, yourself as you are now, walk into the scene. You are now a capable, intelligent, strong adult. You have the ability to care for yourself and to give yourself what you need. Go into the scene and scoop up your younger self and tell them they are the exact opposite of the emotion that has come up. "You are loved. I love you. I accept you. I'm so sorry that happened to you, but I'm here now, and I will never let that happen to you, ever again. I'm here. I'm taking you away from this bad experience. I have you."

Walk with your younger self outside of the movie. It's no longer playing. It's in the past. You can now give yourself everything you need. Keep sitting there a bit longer. Now think about present day challenges you consistently struggle with.

Identify the emotion that comes up for you when these surface-level challenges arise. Is it the same emotion you felt in your movie?

Master Your Mindset

1. Recapture your inner child. Say what you mean. Ask why. Get excited about the things you want. Try. When you fall, get up and try again. Persevere.

2. When you find yourself thinking: *What if it doesn't work?* Switch it to: *What if it does?*

Some Extra Encouragement ...

Moving forward, any time an uncomfortable emotion arises, you can rescue yourself again, right there at that moment. You can take a deep breath when you feel it come on and tell yourself in your mind the opposite of the emotion. You don't have to stop what you're doing and go sit in a room the next time you need to rescue yourself. Maybe you're at the office. Maybe you're at the supermarket. Maybe you're at the Thanksgiving dinner table. You can say a few sentences to yourself in your head to care for yourself in that moment, and you can do this as often as you need.

You are now equipped to care for yourself. You are a capable adult who can now give your younger self what you needed. And when you give yourself what you need, you will never again feel like you're searching. The answers are within you.

That was deep. Still with me? Good job. In the next chapter, we'll go a little deeper, while lightening up a little. Life is meant to be enjoyed. The more inner work you do, the more you open yourself up to enjoy life. Enjoy the next chapter.

Chapter Six

The Answer Is in the Problem

Chapter 6: The Answer Is in the Problem

Change Your Perspective – Change Your Life

> "We don't see others as **they** are. We see others and the world as **we** are."
> ~*Unknown*

What's the problem with problems? The problem is where your focus lies. When you have a problem, you want a solution. Your focus is on finding the solution. But you're looking in the wrong place. The answer is not in the solution; rather, the *solution is in the problem.*

Do you ever notice it's always the same problem that keeps showing up in your life? Maybe it involves different people and different situations, but the problem you find yourself having, the negative emotion it brings up, and the uncomfortable reaction you have to it is the same. Do you ever wonder why? Do you feel like no matter what you do to work on and invest in yourself, you remain stuck or unhappy in a certain area of your life? It's because you have yet to identify the real problem. As discussed in the last chapter, the surface-level challenges keep showing up for a very important reason. They are indicators.

Embrace Discomfort

I bet if you look back through your life, you will see the most pivotal changes that significantly impacted your life, taking you in a better direction, happened at a time when you were at your most uncomfortable. When the problem gets big enough and what you've been doing isn't working, you are forced to look at your problem in a different way.

While I was unhappy at home as a kid, feeling emotionally tormented, it wasn't until I felt my self-esteem tank to an ultimate low that I found the solution to my problem. No matter how uncomfortable I was, I thought my situation was out of my control. But was it? The discomfort squeezed me more and more, and then *a lot* more, until I finally shifted my perspective. My new perspective led to a different reaction. The simple solution, which had been there all along, didn't show up until I chose to see it. When I called my dad and asked if I could come live with him, just like that, I changed my life. I could have asked to move in with him much sooner. But I didn't until the problem became too big for me to handle.

I understand that not all kids who are not doing well in their home environment have the option to make a change like this. That's not the point I'm trying to make. My point is that I *did* have an option, but I didn't see it until I shifted my perspective. Often when you get uncomfortable enough, you see another way that was likely there all along. You just didn't see it before. Instead, you're focused on the painful frustration of your past experiences or looking outside of yourself for understanding and validation. You have the power to shift your perspective, change your reactions, and ultimately uncover the answer. The answer may have always been there; it's *your perspective* that determines whether you see it.

Indicators All Around

When you have a cold, your cough and fatigue get your attention, alerting you to get some rest, some additional fluids, some hot soup. By conserving energy while you rest, your body can heal faster. Your cough and fatigue are not the actual problem. The real problem is the infection. If you had the infection without the symptoms, you wouldn't know something was wrong, and you likely wouldn't give your body the rest it needs. It would take you longer to heal.

When the same problem keeps showing up in your life, leaving you feeling uncomfortable, the surface-level problem is a symptom of the deeper underlying issue. When you begin paying attention to the reoccurring challenges and how you feel around them, then get curious about why, you're on track to uncover the real issue. And when you do, you become equipped to solve it. When your cold clears up, so do your symptoms. In the same way, when you uncover and resolve the root issue that's holding you back, your surface-level problems stop showing up.

The Upside to Problems

Problems can actually be a good thing. The key is to choose a different response. Once you do, you heal and get past the problem. The problem is many of us avoid the problem. You keep your problems around by not addressing them. But when you choose to stay stuck or feeling uncomfortable, this, too, requires uncomfortable effort. Confronting the issue also requires uncomfortable effort. You might as well do the work. The work doesn't have to be as hard as it sounds. The more often you do it, overcoming challenges and finding solutions becomes your life practice, instilling more confidence in your ability to overcome. You become unstoppable. Let's get to it.

Identify the Problem, and You're Almost There

In order for a salesperson to satisfy a customer's need, and inevitably offer a solution in selling their product or service, they must first uncover their customer's problem. They have to dig, ask questions, and research. The hardest part of sales is uncovering the need. But before the sales rep can even begin this process, they first have to be persistent in getting in front of their customer, then take time to gain their trust.

Sales reps also have to be likable. And before they can even begin trying to get in front of and win over their customer, they first have to learn who the decision-maker is, ensuring they have the right audience. Without these key steps, their effort won't produce results. Additionally, they also have to understand and beat out their competitors. If you're not a salesperson and this process sounds extremely challenging, not to worry.

You already know who the decision-maker is: you. Just like you, the customer doesn't want to take time talking about their problem, and they may not even know exactly what their problem is. A skilled sales rep can ask the right questions in the right way to uncover the root problem. As someone trying to solve your own problem, your work is only to uncover the true problem, the root issue that keeps coming up. Sounds much easier, right? Once you allow yourself to observe the indicators that keep showing up as your surface-level challenges, and you choose to get curious about them, you're already choosing a different response. And as we've discussed, different choices bring different outcomes.

How do you stop the bleeding when you don't know where it's coming from? You could try applying pressure to your arm or leg, but if the bleeding is coming from your head, you haven't identified the source of the problem, and you won't fix it.

Changing and creating your life becomes much easier when you pay attention to your emotions and the smaller, persistent challenges that keep showing up. Let them guide you in uncovering the source of the deeper issue. How do you identify these smaller yet consistent problems and uncomfortable challenges? Pay attention to how you're feeling. Just like your physical symptoms show up for an important reason, so that you change something, your emotional triggers are also showing up so that you change something. Often, you ignore the inner signals that are directing you because you're afraid of change. But if you're unhappy in any area of your life, wouldn't a change in that area be better?

If the unknown scares you, I challenge you to ask yourself which is scarier: venturing into the possibility of something greater, or guaranteeing your tomorrow will look exactly as it does today? When you choose the same reaction to the same challenge, you will bring the same result. But what if you shift? When you change the way you look at something, you invite yourself to make a new choice. When you change your perspective, you change your life.

With ability comes responsibility. If you can create the life you want, which could just mean changing the one area where you're feeling stuck, don't you then have a responsibility to yourself to do so? Let's talk about how.

The first part is now a review for you. Pay attention to how you're feeling. Stop and ask yourself, *what's bugging me?* Once you uncover *the what*, go deeper. Why? *Why* is it bothering you? When you sit with how you're feeling and get curious about what's really bothering you and why, and why you always seem to react the way you do, eventually, you uncover the real problem.

It's like getting to the bubble gum in a blow pop or peeling back the layers of an onion. You keep discovering more, and the real discovery is underneath, at the core. You don't find it until you get present and shift your focus from the distractions that have been covering it up. Get present and get curious and allow yourself to focus on the truth, the thing that's not just under your skin, but deeper. It can be scary to look at the problem. The problem hurts. But if you're feeling disruption in a certain area of your life, you're already uncomfortable. Are you uncomfortable enough to make a change?

I encountered another pivotal moment when I was 21. I was dating a guy that I was crazy about. His name was Scott. Scott had this little trick that I found quite impressive. He would grab onto the pole of a stop sign and hold his body perpendicular to it. Scott was attractive, sweet when he wanted to be, and superior to these qualities was the deep connection I felt from the first moment I saw him. This feeling would stick with me for a very long time.

Scott and I both had emotional problems back then. You attract what you are, not what you want, and I had attracted this young man who, while he had a warm heart just like me, was also deeply damaged, just like me. One night, Scott invited me to his apartment for dinner, and we ended up getting into an argument. I became angry and lost my temper, as I often did back then. I slammed his front door on my way out, and as I walked back to my apartment, I noticed something. For the first time, I took a step outside myself and observed my actions, reactions, and behavior. From this new perspective, I noticed that I was not walking back to my apartment; I was stomping. This is the first time I remember becoming *an observer*.

At that moment, I decided to make a change and begin working to control my temper. As my behavior had become a habit, it did take a big effort to change. But I did change. And how I did it was by practicing being an observer. Whenever I began to feel angry and tempted to lose my temper, as I had so many times before, I would catch myself. In observing my emotions, I began to change my reaction to them. The new reaction I chose was not to react. I did this over and over until, eventually, I had a new habit: the habit of controlling my temper. You can change. You can grow. And it usually happens when you get uncomfortable enough. I still think of Scott from time to time, and I wish him happiness.

Another pivotal moment I shared a little about in Chapter One was during my senior year in college. While I had been battling debilitating anxiety attacks since elementary school, suddenly, the problem became bigger. Up until that point, the attacks had been stimulated by certain environments. All of a sudden, they began happening in places I had once felt completely at ease, like the college classroom. The problem grew even bigger on the day I was afraid to leave my apartment for fear that I would have a panic attack in public. I was terrified. I knew I needed help. I had to do something.

I called a friend and asked him to come over. When he got to my apartment, he asked me a question. "What are you afraid of?" he said.

I told him, "I'm afraid of fainting."

"What happens when you faint?" he said.

"I wake up," I said.

Just like that, my perspective began to shift. If the worst thing that happened during the many times I had fainted was that I woke up, what was I truly afraid of? I wasn't afraid of waking up, and inevitably I would.

My friend told me about a book, *The Path to Love* by Deepak Chopra. We walked together on the Plaza in Kansas City to Barnes and Noble, and I bought the book. This was over 20 years ago, so I don't remember everything about the book. But what I do remember learning from the book was that the anxiety leading to my panic attacks was not real. What was happening was the fear that I was *going* to have an attack, ultimately led to an attack. I was creating the panic attacks because I was scared.

If I could somehow not be scared, I wouldn't have a panic attack. How could I then teach myself not to be scared? I could shift my focus, my attention, my perspective. This took practice. Again, I was working to break a habit that I had now been practicing for years. To undo this learning, I began observing myself. Whenever I found myself getting nervous, I would catch myself. I would then shift my focus to something outside of myself. Basically, I would distract myself. I would look around. I would watch people and focus on them. I would focus on my breathing. I would eventually become calmer, the onset symptoms fading, and I wouldn't have an attack.

After a while, the triggers for the attacks also stopped. I had healed myself. But I didn't decide to heal myself, or really even think that there might be a way to heal, until the problem became even bigger. I am grateful for my scariest day.

While you may never have suffered a panic attack, you likely have improved your life in certain areas when things got bad enough.

When you empower yourself by learning that you can create change, what's perhaps even more exciting than the change you've made, is you learn you don't have to let yourself get to the point of unbearable discomfort before you create change sooner. The more you practice this new habit of creating change, the more confidence you instill in yourself that you can. And then what happens is you do it faster. You become happier as you more easily let go of the pain that perhaps once defined you. That's not who you are anymore. You begin manifesting the things you want faster and with less effort.

What if you shift your perspective to view your problems as vehicles for change? On the other side of your challenge lies an opportunity. While it's uncertain how your life will unfold, you can choose your approach to life and problems, and you can ultimately create change.

You have control over your life. What would you like to do? How would you like to feel each day? If there is something you would like to change, are you uncomfortable enough? I now welcome discomfort because the more it gets my attention, I know the closer change is. While I may not know exactly what the change looks like or how it will unfold, just like what's inside a shiny wrapped present, I do know it's going to be great. Are you scared? Whatever your answer is, great. Let's keep going.

Let Your Emotions Lead the Way

A coaching client of mine was having difficulty motivating herself in her job. She reached out, wanting help in holding herself accountable. Accountability was not the real problem. I could see through the context of her message that there was a different issue, and the lack of motivation she felt around her job was the symptom trying to get her attention, alerting her that change was needed. The problem was not that she felt unmotivated. The problem was that her job was not what she felt motivated to do. Remember *the pull* in Chapter One? When you are not listening to and following your pull, you end up feeling disconnected. But the pull is strong; it will keep pulling, and the more you ignore it, the more disconnected and the less happy you feel.

Sometimes you just don't feel like doing something you need to do. Sometimes, once you push through the initial resistance and get started, you surprise yourself with your momentum and keep going. Other times you can benefit from listening to your pull, to what you feel called to do. You take a break to give yourself what you need, and afterward, you have a newfound energy and optimism around what you need to get done. Once you've calmed your mind by giving yourself what you need, you become more focused and accomplish more with less effort.

The moments where you are feeling called away from something you need to do, to something you *want* to do, are smaller pulls that can also be important. They can help you on your path to creating change. The trick is to listen to yourself and pay attention to how you're feeling so you can give yourself what you need. When you let them, your emotions can lead the way toward manifesting with ease. When you ignore or fight against what you want and need, you create unnecessary disruption for yourself.

Sometimes it's bigger than just not feeling like doing something. Sometimes the pull is *pulling* you toward a bigger change. How will you know? Pay attention to how you're feeling. What's the degree of your unhappiness? When you find yourself miserable or even just irritable day after day as you force yourself to continue down a path that no longer aligns with you or maybe never really did, there's a good reason you're feeling miserable. There is something better meant for you. The symptoms of dread, lapsing energy, or frustration are indicators. They are a dead-end in that dark maze, saying, "Don't continue this way. Turn around. Go a different direction." When you pause long enough to let yourself feel your feelings and hear the pull inside of you, the answer becomes clear.

Within the first twenty minutes of the first call with my new client, I learned that she had a special calling, and the time was nearing for her to leave her current job. The job had served its purpose, and it was now time for her to take the confidence she'd gained from her success and trust that she could also be successful doing what was meant for her.

Anytime you are feeling unhappy, growth or change is needed. If where you are and what you're doing is meant for you, you won't feel unhappy. How do you take the first step toward change when you find yourself in a place that no longer fits? Go back to your feelings. Ask yourself, "What do I *feel* like doing?" Start there. The next step is to picture it, to feel it, to see and feel yourself doing what it is you want to be doing. Let yourself get excited and remind yourself to stay focused on the excitement. When fear and doubt creep in, observe the emotion and choose to instead focus on the emotion of excitement. Your state of mind becomes your new direction. Or, your new direction becomes your state of mind, which becomes your life.

Each time I made a significant improvement in my life, this was the exact process I followed, before I even realized it was a process. Remember how discomfort can be a great thing? The first emotion was discomfort, followed by frustration and unhappiness. I paused to let myself feel my feelings and get more curious about them. Then an idea came. Then I got excited and told myself I could do it, and I got started. This process is how I achieve. Most importantly, this process is how I got happy.

I couldn't see all the steps that would show up along my path. In staying curious and excited, I just saw the first step when it appeared. With confidence, I took it, knowing the next step would show up when I was ready. It always did and does, and it will for you too.

Once you go through this process just once, you gain the confidence to know with certainty that you can do it again. And then what happens is you begin to create change easier and faster. You learn you don't have to wait until you're miserable. You can notice you're just a little uncomfortable and quickly implement this process to begin creating change. Take a moment now with this chapter exercise to try it out for yourself.

Chapter 6 Exercise: Identify Your Calling

Part #1: Let's lock in the concept by establishing proof you've already done this. Think of a time in your life when you made a pivotal change, and afterward, you felt happy with the result. Think back to what was happening and how you felt just before making the change. Identify the emotion. Now look back further. Try and remember how long you had been feeling that way before you made a change.

Part #2: Is there something you often feel called to do? What is it? What do you feel like doing right now? Whatever it is that comes to mind, write it down. Identify the emotion you feel when thinking about the thing you want to do. Write down the emotion. Remember it and keep focused on it. Implement this thing you feel like doing into your life a little each week, and if possible, a little each day. Remember to stay excited.

If you have the time and feel focused, give yourself a moment to actively focus on your new goal right now. If you don't yet know your first step, then get present with another activity. It could be an errand, a walk, something on your to-do list, or even getting back to a job that's no longer resonating with you. With your newfound emotion, likely excitement, and trust in yourself that you can make your dream a reality, you will have more energy to focus on your job and other obligations.

Master Your Mindset

1. Pay attention to your emotions. If something is bothering you, sit with it. Allow space to uncover the deeper issue.

2. Give yourself moments to explore what you feel called to do. Create time in your schedule to prioritize what you "feel like doing." The Universe cannot give you more of what you don't take.

3. Remember: When you prove to yourself that you can make a positive change stimulated by discomfort, you will trust your instincts and move faster the next time you feel uncomfortable or unhappy.

Some Extra Encouragement ...

When you're present and excited, your path will show up. Your first step toward achieving the new dream you breathed into existence will show up. You won't even have to look for it. Moving forward, continue giving yourself moments to focus on your endeavor.

If it's getting into better shape, schedule time to work out. If it's starting a new business or a different job, schedule time to research and focus on business planning or job searching.

Just as important as taking action steps toward your goal, is remembering to get excited. Take a few minutes each day to envision yourself doing what you're working toward as if it's already happening. Feel the emotion as if you're doing the thing you want right now. Maybe at first, it's just a few minutes each day where you sit with your eyes closed and envision and feel. It will naturally increase over time. You'll find yourself walking down the street and suddenly smiling as if you're already at the destination.

Chapter Seven

The Way to Win

Chapter 7: The Way to Win

You Succeed at What You Focus On

> "Stay away from those people who try to disparage your ambitions. Small minds will always do that, but great minds will give you a feeling that you can become great too."
> ~*Mark Twain*

Sometimes when you're looking for something but not sure what, you become frantic, floundering as you begin searching in all the wrong places.

I find comfort in a little secret I discovered, and you might too. When you don't know what to do, do nothing. When you don't know what to decide, don't decide. Just keep paying attention to your emotions. Are you beginning to trust them? Let's check in. By now, as you read, you've likely begun listening to your emotions enough to uncover something that's bothering you, and you would like to find a solution. Now I'm asking you to trust yourself and your emotions a bit more. You don't have to know the answer, just follow your feelings. I'll take some pressure off by going first.

Just Like That – An Abrupt Career Change

One hot summer day in Manhattan, my boring business casual clothes sticking to my skin, I dragged myself along First Avenue on the Upper East Side. With my sudden lack of motivation and the humidity not helping, I felt like I was moving through molasses. That day, I didn't have it in me to venture into another customer's office. The value I'd felt in my medical sales job just weeks before had suddenly evaporated, unlike the thick air that day. Overnight, I'd done a 180, going from an overperforming President's Club winning sales rep to that familiar stubborn horse I become when I realize I'm moving in the wrong direction. I'm grateful for her, for this side of my personality, because she was about to change my life for the better, once again.

I knew I needed to move. The little financial safety net I had built was not going to keep me secure for long. With my mostly commission paycheck, my waning motivation was a concern. But which direction? I did find my next direction, just three short weeks from the day I felt hot, bored, and uninspired as I trudged along First Avenue. But first, I began to flounder, looking in all the wrong directions.

My surface-level problem was that I needed another job. I got on LinkedIn and began replying to messages from recruiters who had previously reached out with other medical sales opportunities. My actions made no sense because the problem was not that I needed another medical sales job; it was that I needed to get out of medical sales. Yet, within days I was interviewing for new medical sales jobs. What was I doing? My interviews were not going well as I had no interest in doing the jobs. During a phone interview with another recruiter, I finally stopped myself. "I don't know what I'm doing," I said. "I don't want this job."

This was a good move. I was beginning to listen to myself, to how I was feeling, to what felt right and what didn't. Still, I went on an interview for a Tech Sales position. Great opportunity. Great money. But again, I caught myself. What was I doing? I didn't want the job. What was it I *really* wanted? To find that out and solve my problem, I would have to look elsewhere for the answer. The place to look was within myself. The answers to what you seek are always a thousand times closer than you think. They are within you. As long as you are looking outside yourself, you will forever be searching.

Back to the Hot Summer Day

As I walked along that day, I remember saying to myself out loud, "I need a new job. I have no idea what it is, but I know I need to make at least the same money I make now, and I'm tired of wearing business-casual. I want to wear jeans." I thought about what that might feel like and identified the emotion. It was freedom. I wanted to feel freer.

I conjured up this emotion of freedom as if I were already in my next new job, still having no idea what that might be. I carried this feeling of freedom with me each morning when I woke, and throughout my day, and along with it, a curious excitement about what might unfold. I didn't know what it was, but I knew it would find me. My work was just to stay curious and excited.

At the time, I'm not sure I had fully grasped the concept of what I was doing. Now I employ this process with intention as I fully understand the effectiveness of my actions.

I began putting feelers out and leaning into what felt interesting. Soon, my next opportunity presented itself. Actually, three opportunities presented themselves, and I knew which one was right for me. I chose the riskiest opportunity. It was also the one that provided the most freedom. Had I not stopped to listen to my emotions, I would not have felt the pull, which ultimately led me in a new direction.

Relinquishing Control

If you're someone who likes to understand all the details before making a move, then you're like me, as I shared before. If I have hesitation, there is a reason. I either need more information, or it's an indicator signaling me to move in a different direction. In this way, I keep myself happy. All I have control over is myself, but that's actually a lot.

However, I also understand that there are opportunities waiting for me that even I have yet to imagine. I say *even I* because I'm a dreamer, and no dream is too big. If I stay only with what I know, then I am certain to stay right where I am. I can't know what the road to success will look like, who I will meet along the way or what joys and frustrations will show up. But if I push the dream aside, doing my best to ignore it, and instead stay focused on the same things I focused on yesterday, I do know where I will be in one year from today—the same place, and no closer to the dream that popped into my head for a reason. Even a self-proclaimed control freak can learn to let go, allow, and surrender to the Universe.

It's uncomfortable trying something new for the first time. Yet, without many first times, you would lead a disenchanting life. I remember my first time practicing hot yoga. They call yoga a practice because the work is to keep pushing your body to new limits. As your body feels different each day, your limits will vary each day.

You learn, you practice, and you try your best. Your body begins to know where to go and naturally finds new limits. It's amazing to amaze yourself. If you're not a practicing yogi, having a strong practice does not mean doing every posture perfectly. It means going as deeply as you can into the posture that day while keeping the correct form, and remaining calm and focused in your mind while your heart races.

Having a strong practice means pushing yourself to reach new levels of balanced strength and flexibility. As a result, you become stronger and healthier, and it shows. Yogis typically look years younger than they are. I have now been practicing yoga for 15 years. But there was a first time, and I was a little nervous and a bit uncomfortable because I didn't know what to expect. I thought about trying yoga for nine months before I finally did. At the time, I was a runner. Yoga, I have found, is a great compliment to running, keeping my body conditioned with flexibility and healthier joints so that I'll be able to run for years to come.

There was a first time I tried running too. The freedom I found in that first 800 yards would later become long-distance runs each week. When I'm running, I feel free, inspired, and alone with my thoughts. But there was a first time.

You Succeed at What You Focus On

There was a first time I tried standup comedy as well, which turned into a five-year effort. It's actually something I don't like to talk about much. People have a fascination with comedy and become very curious and inquisitive when you share that you did or do standup. I think people find standup intriguing because most can't see themselves ever doing it. A lot of people think there's nothing scarier than standup comedy. It does take guts, but it's just like anything else. If you want to do it, there's a reason, and so you try.

I often amuse myself with my thoughts and witty conversation inside my head. I'll think, *this would be hilarious in a television show*, and I'll write it down. I decided to take a comedy writing class at a neighborhood comedy club in New York, then I took another one, and then I started doing open mics. Eventually, you get to know people, improve your craft, and get asked to do independently produced shows. This was as far as I got. But if you really put the time in and work it like it's your full-time job, and you have talent, you can move on to get passed at comedy clubs and get regular bookings, leading to travel gigs and tours.

After about a year of dabbling in comedy, maybe doing an open mic once a week, I decided to kick it up a notch and invest more time. A year or two later, I started thinking, if you tried harder, maybe you could be really good. I started trying harder. I was now doing five open mics a week. I'd do a couple during the week after work and then fill my Saturdays and Sundays with back-to-back open mics in the Village. I improved. People would come up to me after a mic or a show and tell me I was funny and sometimes ask me to be in their show. It felt rewarding.

America's Got Talent was in town holding auditions, and I went. I performed a great set, and after everyone in my group had gone, we were instructed to wait outside. A moment later, the lady came out and called my number. I followed her back into the big conference room. It was just her and me. She told me I was the funniest comedian she'd seen all day, and she wrote her email down on a piece of paper and asked me to send her some clips of my performances. I'll come back to this story later and share what transpired. I kept the paper with her email address on it. I still have it years later. I don't think about it often, but I know right where it is, and it's a reminder of how quickly your life can change and that you succeed at what you focus on.

You can do this for yourself as well. Think about an achievement you're proud of. Maybe the promotion you got or the delicious meal you made for your date. Maybe you crossed a big project off your to-do list. Checking off a task on your to-do list might seem small, but it's not. I take little moments all throughout the day, every day, to celebrate myself and my accomplishments. I smile and tell myself, "good job," even for the littlest things. This reinforces the drive to be productive, instills a sense of accomplishment in your ability to complete things, and builds momentum to carry you further and with less effort. We'll discuss more on this later. For now, brainstorm a few more things you did that you're proud of. Take two minutes to do that now. Write them down.

***

Okay, you're back. Revisiting some of your past achievements and holding the sense of accomplishment you are likely now feeling, ask yourself *how* you achieved what you did. I know the answer too, and I'll tell you. You focused on it. That's it. Focus. You succeed at what you focus on.

The Law of Attraction

Good or bad, positive or negative, success or defeat, you succeed at what you focus on. Where your attention goes, you go. If you're entering into a new relationship you're excited about yet scared it will fail because your focus is on your past relationships that didn't work out, forming your belief that *this relationship won't work out either*, that's your focus. Your thoughts are your focus. Your focus forms your beliefs. Your beliefs influence your actions or inaction, which ultimately shapes your outcomes. If your focus is *"it won't work,"* then it won't.

If this concept is true for negative outcomes, wouldn't it then be just as true for positive outcomes? If your thought is, "I'm going to make $200,000 this year," your focus will be on making $200,000. Your focus will influence your actions, and you will take the first step toward reaching your goal. Keeping your focus on the goal, your belief in yourself, and your excitement, you will build momentum, quickly identify the next step, and take action.

This is how successful people operate. They tell themselves they can. Success is a mindset. Successful people listen to their emotions and follow their instincts. The opportunities are there, waiting to be seized. But first, you must be on the path. You must be moving. I'm envisioning Super Mario chomping on a mushroom in the game by Nintendo. Mario cannot get the mushroom unless he's moving.

Can life really be this simple? I think so. If you're on your path, you can get the prize, even prizes you've not yet imagined. Your path is waiting. If you're not sure how to find your path, then you're not listening to yourself.

Success Starts with State of Mind

State of Mind: *your mood or mental state.*

If you don't like where you are in your life or a particular area of your life, consider shifting your focus to new possibilities. If successful people tell themselves they can, why not start telling yourself *you can and you will*? What do you have to lose? Try it and observe the shift in your emotions. How you feel influences your focus and your habits. Your world, your life, is the domino effect you produce, starting with your thoughts. If you want to change your life, you must change your state of mind.

If you want to change your state of mind, you must change your thoughts. Start with the thought, *"What if I can? What might that be like?"* Lead with the emotion of curiosity over worry, get excited, and then get going. What if you're excited about getting started on your idea but have to go to work? Simple. Go to work. Get present with your day while carrying the newfound positive energy you're now vibrating in. What will happen is you will get an idea, which will be your first step, and you'll be ready to come back to it a little later after your workday.

You will see the step because you're present; you're in a state of excitement. Remember, you succeed at what you focus on. If you're focused on how much you hate your job, this will be your state of mind, which will keep you stuck. But what if you shift your focus to dreaming about what you actually want to be doing? Your focus has changed, and therefore, *you* will change.

Successful people focus on the problem rather than avoiding it. What's really bothering them and why? It's hard work, and just like any new experience, it will feel uncomfortable at first. But if you're unhappy, you are uncomfortable, so what's the difference? The difference is the discomfort you know versus the discomfort you don't know. Whichever you choose, you are predicting your future. You are in control. What do you want for yourself?

There are many reasons you might be scared to look within the deep, dark, mysterious place inside yourself. One reason is you will likely uncover some old wounds that need tending to. Another reason is once you identify a problem, or the solution, then you have to make the choice to either do something about it and risk trying and failing, or live with the fact that you are lying to yourself by not pursuing what it is you truly want. Doesn't this last option sound really bad? If your answer is "yes," why even let it be an option?

Power in Letting Go

Successful people know how and when to create distance. When you find yourself pushing for more, you will inevitably encounter others who try to discourage you. Know that when someone tells you about yourself, they are often talking about themselves, especially if they are telling you that you can't. It's not that they don't believe you can do it; they don't believe *they* can do it. Your willingness to overcome fear and choose to try forces them to look in the mirror, admitting there's perhaps something more they want for themselves. Your courage is a big, bold reminder that they are choosing not to live up to their potential. Their motive in discouraging you is not even to make you feel bad. The reason, of which they are likely unaware, is that if they succeed in discouraging you from trying, in essence, it brings you down to their level, a place they can understand.

If you pay attention, you will likely notice that the people who believe in themselves and actively and excitedly engage in their pursuits also believe in others. They encourage others. While those who adopt a different attitude, who aren't trying and believing in themselves, discourage others from their pursuits. It can sometimes be important to let these people go while you work toward your goals, or at least to create some distance. This is not a selfish act because in order to give your best to those around you, you must be your best. In order to be your best, you must build yourself up by first giving to yourself.

A wise woman once told me, in different words, that a positive person cannot sustain a negative person and vice versa. The positive-minded person will always try to bring up the negative-minded person, while the negative person will always try to bring down the positive person. This is because they are attempting to get on the same level. I have also learned this to be true through many of my own experiences. Ever since I was very little, I always believed in myself and that I could achieve whatever I set out to. I inherently knew this to be true before I even understood what it is to dream. As a result, I always tried.

I listened to how I was feeling. When I liked something, I kept at it. And when I didn't, my mind and body adamantly shut down. This is actually a useful skill to learn to activate if you're not already, as it helps you align your focus. It helps you prioritize. And remember, you succeed at what you focus on. We'll discuss more on that and how sometimes *quitting is actually winning* later in the chapter.

A clairvoyant even once told me that my gift is my awareness that the world is my oyster, and that I will be helping others to learn this for themselves. How about that? Years later, my calling became increasingly pronounced. But ever since I was very little, I always encouraged others, "yes, you can," and tried to get them to believe in themselves. When you believe in yourself so much, you naturally have the same belief in others. I always encouraged my friends, who often came to me seeking advice.

Thinking positively and trying and encouraging others came naturally to me. After our conversations, my friends would come away saying, "You're so inspirational. You always help me so much." One time, I remember thinking, "Actually, no, I'm not helping you at all." I would encourage, uplift, and share relevant real-life stories and examples, yet their situation never changed. Year after year, the same friends would come to me with the same problems. After a while, I noticed it was growing exhausting.

The relationships were unbalanced. While I was trying to bring them up, they weren't budging. And while they weren't attempting to bring me down, I began to feel drained after a while as I wasn't receiving in these friendships. The energy balance did not align, and after years, I ended these friendships with no regrets. I'm sure some of my former friends may think my actions harsh. However, I tried for years to level the playing field of our connections. It was time to walk away and keep more of my energy for myself. I had places I wanted to go, which required my energy and creativity. The less energy I have for myself, the less I have to give to others. I learned that I am meant to share my energy, positive mindset, and encouragement in a different capacity and on a broader scale. And by letting go of these unbalanced relationships, I had more time and energy to create. I felt better, and I began generating ideas more quickly.

After I had gone into business for myself, I was talking with an acquaintance. She said, "I think the government should give out small business loans to women because I want to start my own business."

"So, start your own business," I said with a genuine smile on my face. "You can do it."

A positive trying to bring up a negative does not work. This is what she said: "You're not Wonder Woman. You need help too." This was when I stopped talking. It didn't matter what I said. She didn't believe in herself, so naturally, she didn't believe in me. Except, I knew that I was Wonder Woman. I had already started my own business, not needing any help from the government or anyone else. I certainly didn't need any help for the sole fact that I'm a woman. Women and men are strong when they choose to be. I choose to believe in myself, which makes me strong. It also drives my insatiable belief in others. I know without a doubt that you are capable of anything you set your mind to. The trick is in the mind.

When Quitting Is Winning

Can believing in yourself ever be a bad thing? Sure. When you believe in yourself without a doubt that you can and will succeed, yet you're focused in the wrong direction. It is then that quitting can be winning.

Here's what happened with my standup comedy win and the follow-up email to my America's Got Talent contact. I was impressed with myself that I had put in more effort and focus on my comedy, and as a result, I had succeeded. I did well on my audition, and she wanted to move me forward. My task was to send her some additional recordings of my sets.

I got started looking back through my material, which wasn't that great. Had I truly been excited to keep going in the direction of standup comedy, I would have hustled to quickly book a couple of shows where I could tape some new material, or at least continued practicing and gotten in some solid performances at some open mics that I could tape and send to her. But I wasn't truly excited. I had almost no motivation to do this, and I didn't get it together. I did email her some of my sets, but they were mediocre at best, and the process ended there.

Deep down, or not even that deep down, I knew a career in standup comedy was far from what I wanted. Here's how I knew: I'm not a night person. I don't enjoy being in comedy clubs or bars late at night, which is primetime comedy hour. I don't like traveling. If you're building a career in comedy and you get a booking, you better go, or you're not getting invited back. I didn't even like taking the train to Long Island to do a show.

While I'm very outgoing, I'm actually an introvert. I require a lot of alone time to re-energize. The necessary networking before, during, and after comedy shows to stay plugged into the community and get additional opportunities, exhausted me. I found myself fantasizing about getting home even before heading out to a show. In short, I hated doing standup. Yet, for five years, I had been putting increasing energy into it. While I was improving, I was going further in a direction that was not meant for me. And I knew it wasn't meant for me because plain and simple: I didn't like it. It was time to quit. I don't like to give up. I wondered what I'd do with all the extra time. While initially, I felt the bittersweet defeat of giving up, I quickly found a new focus with which I felt happier and aligned.

Giving up is winning when it's not your path. And walking away is winning when a relationship depletes rather than energizes you. Successful people know how and when to let go. If a friend or a job, or a pastime is taking your focus while leaving you with less, it's time to give up. How can you know? By paying attention to your emotions. Take a moment. Take a breath. And ask yourself how you're feeling. Whatever the emotion is around the person or situation, there's your answer.

That right there is how to never make another mistake. Are there really any mistakes? Perhaps not. There are lessons, which make you stronger, but only if you learn and apply them. Sometimes it takes a while to learn, and that's okay. You will get another opportunity. Pay attention. You will notice the same problem keeps showing up in different ways until you choose a different reaction. This solves the problem, and it stops showing up. While there may not be true mistakes, there are delays on your path. But the better you get at listening to yourself and your emotions and then changing your reactions, you learn to let go more quickly of what does not align. You seize new directions faster, naturally moving toward what you want with less effort.

Successful people have mastered the art of believing in themselves, prioritizing their focus, letting go, and investing in themselves. In the next chapter, we'll discuss why you are your most important investment. First, take a moment to complete the chapter exercise. Remember, learning is one thing. But the application, the action, is what leads to new things.

Chapter 7 Exercise: Identify What's Bugging You and Let Go

Consider what it might be time to let go of in your life. Take a moment to sit and think about how you're feeling. What's bugging you? See what surfaces and what it might be time to let go of. Write down what comes to mind. Take a moment to consider the emotion that surfaces around what you're considering letting go of. Do you want to carry this emotion with you into your future? Let your answer fuel your motivation to take action.

Master Your Mindset

1. Quitting is winning. Does your energy soar or sink at the thought of your job or a current obligation? Your direction (toward or away) is in how you're feeling.

2. Pay attention to how you feel around people. If you feel depleted rather than energized, it may be time to walk away.

3. When you keep encountering the same problem, consider changing your reaction. When you respond in a new way, you will create a new experience.

Some Extra Encouragement ...

Remember that when you let go of what no longer serves you, you create space for something new to come in. While perhaps uncomfortable at first, it gets easier. Letting go helps you create a life that feels fulfilling and better aligned. Letting go is an investment in yourself.

Chapter Eight

Your Most Important Investment

Chapter 8: Your Most Important Investment

You Project How You Feel about Yourself, Get Feeling Good

"Give a man a fish, and he will eat for a day. Teach a man to fish, and he will eat for a lifetime."

~ *Lao Tsu*

The greatest investment you will ever make is the one you make in yourself. If you think that sounds selfish, consider that how you conduct yourself and how you feel about yourself directly impacts those around you. This outward ripple effect you create extends far beyond what you can see. It's energy, and we are all connected.

Have you ever had someone on your mind, and then out of the blue, they call you, or you run into them? Have you ever met someone and felt an instant connection, having never before spoken? Have you ever had someone with whom you've lost touch, increasingly on your mind, and you later learned they were sick? Have you started your day in a good mood, and then someone bumped into you, and hurried on their way without an apology? With your mood now shifted, did you then choose to let the elevator door close on the next person rushing to catch it, or maybe consider doing so?

As humans, we feel each other's energy and often carry the impending vibration. But you have choices. You can become conscious observers, choosing to have a positive impact on those around you. This gets easier when you feel good on the inside.

I have heard that women, more so than men, can be quite affected by the energy of others. This makes sense as most women are naturally more in touch with their emotions. Girls are raised with the perception that expressing how they feel is okay, while boys are often taught to show their strength by hiding emotion. I have a very strong tendency to pick up on and, if I'm not careful, absorb the emotional energy of those around me. As my generally good mood can shift, I choose my company and surroundings carefully.

When You Give Away Your Resources, You Run Out

Once upon a time, a brilliant and bright-eyed young woman believed in herself. She emigrated to the U.S. from a small European country on a work program. She successfully completed the program, which involved a long bus ride and then a long walk to work in the freezing cold during wintertime. She went on to complete her MBA at NYU and landed a job on Wall Street, where she also lived in an upscale high-rise apartment. She invited me there sometimes, and we'd drink wine on her rooftop overlooking the city. She made it. Wouldn't you say?

I might also mention that my friend is a genius, her IQ tipping over the edge, declaring her so. Not only is she smart and ambitious, but she's also creative, talented, and a dreamer, as she often shared ideas for new business ventures.

Chapter 8: Your Most Important Investment

While I scored reasonably well on my IQ test, I would have scored better if I didn't spend the first 15 minutes of the timed test figuring out what was going on. While I effortlessly understand others' feelings and motives better than they sometimes do themselves, logically piecing physical elements together like constructing a shelf or a new way to rearrange furniture is not my strong suit. On the other hand, my friend's brain quickly and effortlessly maps out numbers, processes, and systems, and without any training. How did a literally brilliant and accomplished dreamer end up with no other option than to go back to where she started? Simple. She stopped putting herself first.

One day her cousin came from abroad for a visit, a two-week stay with my friend in her Manhattan studio apartment. Only she had no intentions of ever leaving or of supporting herself. In addition to my friend's 80-hour work weeks, she now took on the daunting obligation of supporting her perfectly capable family member.

Her cousin quickly found a job, and she just as quickly found an excuse to quit. Years later, my friend was still supporting her cousin for a stay extending far beyond two weeks. My friend grew exhausted. She became overwhelmed, and fearful, scared to quit her job on Wall Street in pursuit of the bigger goals she once dreamed of. I might also add that she was not treated well in her job, often loaded up with 15-hour workdays while her colleagues vacationed. Her self-esteem further plummeted each year she was passed over for promotions while watching her teammates move up the ladder. How we do anything is how we do everything. If you are letting someone take advantage of you in one area of your life, it's likely happening in another.

On her rooftop, Manhattan's inspiring city lights enveloping us, I listened to my friend complain about her job and how she had hated it for five years. I watched her once vibrant spirit diminish as she grew further away from the confident woman I first met. I watched her family instill fear in her, discouraging her while she worked, and they didn't. She supported them, not just one, but now two family members who had come to stay with her in her now one-bedroom apartment she'd gotten to accommodate them. My gentle encouragement and honest viewpoint of her situation were not what she was ready to receive.

She finally quit her job one day, no longer able to take the mental abuse. Her confidence now deflated; she never looked for another job. Months later, with no money coming in, she and her family packed up their things and moved back to their home country in Europe.

Intelligence is not what leads to success. It's mindset and belief in oneself that carries you further. When my friend was operating within an abundance mindset, one where she believed in herself, she succeeded. She landed the work program. She moved to the U.S. She successfully completed the work program. She moved to New York. She completed her MBA. She landed a job on Wall Street and moved into a luxury highrise. The average American does not do this. But she did. And later, when she shifted her mindset from believing in herself to doubting herself, and started putting others before herself, she depleted her resources and her confidence. How did she help her family in the end by putting them first?

Guilt Serves No Purpose

"They are my family. This is our culture. They are my responsibility," she would say. When you choose to care for someone else who is perfectly capable of caring for themselves, you are not only enabling them but showing them you don't believe in them. You are saying, "*I don't believe you can do it, so I will do it for you.*" You only have control over yourself. You can help others by being an example, by leading your life with fearless belief in yourself. You can approach your dreams with curiosity. "What if it *does* work?"

As we discussed earlier in the book, vibrations that do not align either adjust to come together, or they fall apart. But unaligned energies cannot remain. In this struggle for energy alignment, one of two things happens: the positive person gives up on trying to help the negative person and walks away, choosing to invest in the only thing they really have control over—themselves. Or, they become increasingly exhausted and shrink to align with the lower energy vibration. When you instead lead by example, investing in yourself, you have more to offer those around you.

Your Choices Become Your Habits, Become Your Mood, Becomes Your Life

Regardless of your tendencies to be impacted by others, you do have choices. Your choices create your life. If you don't like your life, try making some different choices. You will see a difference, and quickly.

Think back to a morning that did not start off so great for you. Maybe you overslept; you rushed through your first cup of coffee and burnt your tongue. The outfit you threw on wasn't right for the weather. You arrived late to work, and now a little sweaty and wrinkled. Likely, in this scenario, you're not vibrating in your best energy. What can you do about this? You can choose to get yourself in check before anything else goes wrong with your day.

You are in control. You are creating this day, and that's empowering. What kind of day do you want to create? You can choose to focus on what's not perfect, going deeper down the unpleasant rabbit hole that was the start of your day, or you can observe how you're feeling, and make a choice to focus for a moment on something in your life you feel good about. Instantly, your state of mind will shift to gratitude. Which way would you like your dominos to fall?

How do you catch yourself from tumbling down the wrong side of the domino effect? The first thing you do is the most impactful, and it's also the easiest.

When you find yourself thinking negative thoughts, unless you get yourself in check and quickly, one negative thought leads to the next, which creates your mood. Suddenly you're walking around in a negative energy and attracting more negative experiences. Have you ever found yourself replaying past arguments in your head, maybe even recalling something that happened years back? Before you know it, rather than being in the present moment, you're in your head creating a scene and a new argument that never happened and becoming even angrier than you were at the first thought of the memory.

When you're not present, you will surely miss out on opportunities. If I'm stuck in my head thinking about a past relationship that didn't work out, and I'm focused on how nothing ever works out for me in relationships, I won't notice the cute, successful, single guy at the other end of the subway who would actually love to meet his future wife. He won't notice me either because our energies don't match. The thing I want is not the thing I *am* in that moment. My choice to focus on a negative memory rather than enjoy the possibility of the present has created a missed opportunity.

Alternatively, if I wake up and the first thing I do is start thinking about the bad relationship from the past, I can catch myself. I can *observe* myself. What is my emotion, and where is my focus? If it's not in a good place, I can shift it. I can choose to think of something I appreciate that I already have and take on the emotion of gratitude, and work to keep my focus there. This simple process that takes seconds does require effort, but it does work, and it is a choice.

The next time you find yourself thinking a negative thought or feeling a negative emotion, catch yourself. Observe without judgment and then make a choice. Choose to observe your experiences and your interactions. Aren't you more likely to receive a smile when you give a smile? When you shift your perspective, can you see how easy it can be to create the life you want? And aren't you worth it?

When I wake up each morning, I choose my focus. I can choose to focus on what is missing in my life, or I can choose to focus on how grateful I am for my first cup of rich, delicious French press coffee. I can focus on this emotion of gratitude and choose to carry it with me as I start my day. I can choose to feel curious and excited about the unknown that lies ahead.

For the first half of my adult life, I chose the former perspective. Each day I woke, I put my focus on the things that weren't working out in my life, and while I still chose positive activities and invested in myself each day, I still felt bad, attracting more negative experiences. When I changed my focus, I changed my life.

On occasion, I'll still catch myself focusing on something from the past that bothered me. But before I let my thoughts tip the dominos into a downward spiral, I observe. I catch myself, and I smile to myself, aware that I can shift my mood with a thought. And then I do, which brings an even bigger smile with the awareness of just how powerful I truly am.

When you recognize your power to make choices, you learn that you can manifest what you want. You're no longer looking outside yourself for happiness. This is life-changing, and anyone has this power, including you.

When *you* change, your experiences change, not the other way around. This is what the gurus mean when they say, "You attract what you *are* and not what you *want*." Why would someone in a healthy frame of mind want to spend time with or even approach someone vibrating in an off-putting energy? If you don't like what you're attracting, the place to look is within.

We don't all get along with everyone. There will be people you align with and people you don't. When your energy is out of alignment, you then align with people and things that don't feel good. I used to have a lot of negative experiences and often attracted negative energy. To try and protect myself, I kept my guard up. Once I began to work on myself, my outward experiences changed. I no longer needed to keep myself protected against bad energy. I just wasn't attracting these experiences. The better I felt within, the better my outward experiences.

Where to start? Start by observing your emotions.

You are your Most Important Investment

Why would anyone choose not to invest in themselves? Let's take a closer look at guilt. Taking on the feeling of guilt is taking on an emotion of feeling bad about oneself. You can feel guilty that you ate an extra cookie. You can feel guilty that you love your job while your partner feels dissatisfied with theirs. You can feel guilty for mistreating someone in the past. You can feel guilty for overreacting.

If you succeed at what you focus on and your focus is on feeling guilty, you will breed more discontent. Feelings of guilt keep you stuck. You can't change the past. But when you change your present mindset, choosing to adopt a positive emotion and outlook, you do change your future. You can hold onto guilt, focusing on what you did or didn't do, and manifest more of the same in your future. Who is your guilt serving? Not yourself and not those around you. I practice not harboring any guilt by simply saying "I'm sorry" when I'm not happy with my actions, and then I try to do better moving forward. That's it.

Whatever you do to make yourself feel good, to invest in yourself, you will be that much better to those around you. When I give myself time to go for a run, I feel better and am kinder to others. Keeping my body feeling great, my mind is focused and I'm more efficient. When you feel unhappy, your mind is distracted. Your attention is divided between the person or task you're trying to focus on, while also trying to work out a problem in your head in an attempt to feel better. But when you keep yourself feeling good, the distraction eliminates itself. There will always be more work to get done and people who need you, and you will give them your best when you feel your best.

Become a Wise Investor

As you attract more of how you're feeling, it's imperative to keep yourself vibrating in positive energy. This means taking time to invest in yourself by doing what feels good to you. The choice to invest in yourself has power far beyond the moment you choose to do so. When you want something new or different in your life, the only way you will have the time for it is if you *give* yourself time. Remember the power of your choices? You choose what you prioritize.

Now that you've learned to listen to your emotions and to trust your instincts, you are ready to make yet another powerful choice—the choice to honor yourself by investing in yourself. You've also learned that you succeed at what you focus on. If you skip the gym to help a neighbor, your focus is not on prioritizing your health and fitness goals, and while you will still be a nice neighbor in a year, you won't feel any better about your physical health and about how you feel when you look in the mirror.

If you choose to keep investing 50 hours a week toward bringing home your overtime pay, you will still be in your same job a year later and no closer to getting your new business idea off the ground. If instead, you choose to set aside two hours a day to invest in your goals, researching, planning, and dreaming, by the end of that year, you will have focused a full month of hours toward them. Will you have made progress?

You can choose success by choosing to focus on what feels meaningful to you. As you have the power to prioritize your focus, you are the only one who can ever hold yourself back. View ideas that energize and excite you as opportunities. It's up to you to take the first step. When you choose not to, out of guilt that you're not doing for someone else, or fear that you won't finish obligations, you will never reach the finish line. You will never succeed at your goal. If you don't choose to take the first step, the second cannot show up.

Choose your focus. Let go of guilt. The people who are meant to be in your life and on your path will benefit from what you have to offer, which you won't discover to your full capacity without taking time to invest in yourself. If something feels meaningful, it's for a reason. When you give yourself one hour to invest in yourself, the Universe can then give you two. Bringing yourself into greater alignment, you also begin vibrating in an increasingly positive energy. You naturally become more focused and accomplish more in less time and with less effort.

Creating Time

Take a look at your life and where you are today. Let's quickly revisit something discussed earlier in the book. Think of one of your accomplishments or something you feel proud of. How did you get there? You focused on it, and you succeeded. Let the example you came up with instill confidence in yourself that you can and will succeed at what you choose to focus on.

How do you make time when there is not enough time? Schedule time. While each day seems to fly by faster than the next, this doesn't change the fact that there are still a lot of hours in each day. It's what you do with your hours that either takes you where you want to go or keeps you where you are. Just as you schedule time to work and sleep, you can also schedule time to focus on your new endeavor. Whether it's taking up a fitness regimen, researching your new business idea, or going for walks to clear your head and practice presence, it's up to you to schedule time.

If you're not yet comfortable prioritizing yourself, try thinking of it like this: if you respect the time you set aside to invest in yourself, those around you will have no choice but to respect it as well, and eventually, they will. No one questions the time you devote to work each day, making dinner, or running your errands. In the same way you prioritize everything you currently do, if there is a new direction you wish to explore, this direction is now a priority.

At first, stepping away from work to go for a run at lunchtime, for example, may feel uncomfortable. But if you're ready to create change, you must make it happen. Set aside the time, give that time to yourself, and eventually, it will become just what you do. You will notice you feel happier, more fulfilled, and present. Then when it's time to get back to work or laundry or whatever you *have* to do, you will feel more focused, complete the task faster, and even enjoy it more. By *taking* time, you just created time.

You will also notice that what naturally begins to happen is the two hours you set aside to focus on your goal, some days become four, increasing over time, until you have changed your life. But you have to start somewhere. Just get started, even if it's one hour a day. Commit to that one hour. Give that to yourself. What do you want to succeed at? Once you say it out loud, you've breathed life into your goal, and you're halfway there. The hardest part is getting started, showing up. It is your responsibility to show up for yourself. No one else can do that for you, which means no one else can take that from you.

How to Identify Your Purpose

What if you haven't yet found what you want? That thing you truly feel in your element when doing? That thing you're really good at doing in the way only you can? Not sure what's pulling you or where to? My advice here is the same—give yourself moments.

You know those times when you really just feel like doing something? Maybe you planned to get a jump start on your taxes, but now you really just feel like watching a movie. Maybe you're in the middle of your workday, and you really just feel like stepping out for a walk around the block and an ice cream cone. Do you ever think there might be a very good reason you feel like doing something? Could your desire be your intuition? Your intuition is there not only to protect and keep you safe, but also to guide you in the right direction. You never know where your instincts might lead you.

One evening I went to my favorite neighborhood spot to get a glass of wine and change of atmosphere. I always see people I know there, and this time was no different. I walked in, and right away, a friend across the bar waved me over to join him and his company. I said hello and visited for a moment, but for some reason, I didn't feel like sitting there. There was no logic behind it, but I felt like sitting in the middle of the bar and not at the end in the corner. I had sat in that corner many times before and liked that seat, but that night I just didn't feel like sitting there. I decided to go with what I felt and take a different seat.

I later struck up a conversation with a gentleman sitting next to me. Like myself, he had been there many times before. Yet, I had never seen him. He asked me what I did to keep busy during Covid, and I told him I was working on some writing projects. He seemed unusually interested in a TV show idea I was working on as he kept asking more questions about it. After I told him more about the show, he took out his card and handed it to me. This man worked at NBC Universal. "Email me your script," he said. "I'll read it and let you know what I think." In doing what I felt like, which was just choosing a bar seat, I had created an opportunity.

Your life can change in a moment. You never know what's around the corner. When you take notice of what you feel like doing, then take action, even when it seems insignificant or illogical, you are often on the right track. There is no way for you to know what's ahead unless you always choose the same thing.

You can easily feel your next step when you're present and paying attention to your emotions. How are you feeling? What do you feel like doing? What's striking your curiosity? Just as you can create new experiences and the life you want by listening to and doing more of what you feel like, you can also keep yourself from unnecessary painful experiences. We'll talk about this in the next chapter.

Choosing the Right Career Path

Do you love your job? Do most of the people you know love their jobs? When you don't love what you're doing, it's because something better is meant for you. The lack of energy and motivation around what you're dragging yourself to do is the indicator. It's the blinking signal telling you to turn. This direction doesn't feel good; turn left. There's something better worth exploring over there. When you trust your intuition, telling you which way is right for you, you move toward your destiny with ease. Still, many people don't. You can make choices, or you can make excuses.

Your job is where you spend most of your time. If you don't like it, consider asking yourself why you're spending most of your life focused in an area that doesn't feel right? Fear of the unknown? By applying the concepts we've discussed throughout the book, you can overcome fear and experience greater happiness, success, and abundance.

Who defines success? You do, for yourself, no one else. I think the biggest measure of success is happiness. Whatever truly makes you feel happy when you're doing it, that's success.

It can be scary to leave behind the security of what you know and venture down a path you cannot yet see the end of. But ask yourself how you're feeling when you go to work. How do you feel when you're doing the things you do every day? How do you feel around the people you spend time with? If your answer to any of these questions is "not very good," there is your indicator. It's time for a change.

If you think you feel secure in keeping with what you know when you feel unhappy or unfulfilled, is that really security?

Chapter 8 Exercise: Identify your Direction

Now that you're further into the book and perhaps can more easily apply the concepts we've discussed, let's revisit an earlier question to see if something new shows up.

Take a moment here to be honest with yourself. Sit with your eyes closed and bring yourself present with some deep breathing and any other breathing exercises you like. Try to keep your mind focused on the present moment, hearing the sounds around you. After a few minutes and once you're feeling calm and relaxed, ask yourself the *"If I could do anything"* question. If failure were not possible and money were not an issue, what would you do? What would your life look like? How would it feel? Picture it in your mind's eye.

Did you take some time to complete your mediation? If so, you're ready to move on. If not, go back and complete your meditation now. I'll be right here waiting for you. Remember, you have choices, and the choices you make dictate the life you create for yourself.

Choosing to take a moment to sit with yourself and go inward to meditate is a choice to invest in yourself. If the newness of meditation is a struggle for you, remember: new choices bring new outcomes. You can empower yourself by stepping in the direction of the life you want for yourself right now, at this moment. I'll meet you back here after your meditation; whether it takes you 20 minutes or an hour, I'll be here.

* * *

You've completed your meditation. Either a new direction or idea has surfaced, or maybe a thought that sparks your curiosity. It can be as simple as something that pops into your mind that you'd like to research and learn more about. Now what? This part is easy. Your only job is to get excited and curious about your new idea. Get curious about how you feel when you're actively doing this thing you want to be doing, then get curious about how it will happen. Don't *worry* about how it will happen. Wonder and worry are very different emotions. Choose wonder.

Write down your new goal or your new idea. Successful people write down their goals. What does the action of writing down your goals actually do?

- It makes them real, giving you a responsibility to act on them. Responsibility is good. You take care of things you are responsible for. Responsibility gives you purpose.

- It improves your focus.

Think about how you feel when you write out your *To-Do* lists. If this is not a common practice for you, start making it one now. When you have eighteen ideas or tasks swimming around your head, you can feel overwhelmed and stressed. You are in your head during these times, which means you are not focused or present. When you take a moment to move the tasks or ideas out of your head and onto a piece of paper, you feel better. Even if it's not yet time to focus on the goal, you know it's there to come back to when you're ready.

Master Your Mindset

1. The more you invest in yourself, the more you have to offer others.

2. The happier you feel, the less distracted and more efficient you are.

3. When you write down your goals, they become real, and you create a responsibility to work toward them.

4. To-do lists are powerful. Get your tasks out of your head and onto paper. This act frees and focuses your mind.

Some Extra Encouragement ...

We discussed earlier how you can give yourself what you need emotionally. Similarly, you can also give yourself time to focus on what is calling you. Meditate to give yourself an opportunity to identify what that is. Uncover your idea. Get excited and get curious.

Write down your goal. Then get present. Schedule time to focus on your goal for one hour each day or even an hour every other day. You will notice that you're vibrating in a more positive state afterwards. Your increased energy turns into momentum, heightening your focus around your obligations. This is how you create time, move toward achieving your goals, and grow your confidence in yourself that, "yes, you can."

A new mindset leads to new habits, leading to a healthier and happier *you*—the *you* you were always meant to be. Now you can see that you are no different than someone you perceive as more successful than you. Success is a mindset. Success is a choice.

It's time to lock in what you've learned with a bonus chapter exercise.

Adopt your new mindset and success habits by practicing them each day. Take a few minutes for yourself, preferably in the morning, to start your untouched day in the most positive way possible. It can be as little as fifteen minutes or as much as an hour. Take this time to meditate and get vibrating in the most positive energy possible.

Some days will be better than others, and that's okay. Take time to go within and remind yourself of your dreams, goals, and where you're heading. Touch the feeling of whatever that dream feels like as if it is actually happening right now. Get excited. Get curious. Be grateful as if you've already achieved it. Then get more excited. Then open your eyes, get present, and get started with your day. Write down any new ideas that came up during your meditation. When you are in the present moment, you are in a state of creation, and you will notice the ideas coming.

Acknowledging your goals requires vulnerability, admitting there is something you want. In the next chapter, we'll go deeper into the importance of being vulnerable, what it means, and how it can enrich your life. See you in the next chapter.

Chapter Nine

Vulnerability

Chapter 9: Vulnerability

Your Greatest Strength Lies within Your Vulnerability

"Asking for help is not a weakness. Asking for help is a superpower, and men, especially us."
~*The Rock*

Vulnerability: capable of being physically or emotionally wounded.

If being vulnerable exposes you to the opportunity of getting hurt, how can being vulnerable be the key to strength?

I believe one thing people all have in common; whether you live in a democracy or a dictatorship, whether you dine at four-star restaurants or on food stamps, whether you are four years old or eighty-four years old, is the desire to be understood, maybe not by everyone, but by someone. Why do you argue your point? Why do you share your stories? Why do you strike up conversation? Why do you take pleasure in sharing an inside joke? Why do you choose just one person to come home to, one best friend, or cherish that special connection with your most favored relative? The answer to all these questions is in just one word. Connection.

Connection feels good, really good. Yet, it doesn't exist without risk. You know the saying, *"With great risk comes great reward."* The bigger payoff comes with the commission-only job, as there is the risk you might make nothing. On the other hand, there's little to no risk in a salary job, but it's highly unlikely that you'll earn a colossal payout for your performance that month.

What do you risk in a connection? The only way to have a real connection is to open up and let someone see you, to have the courage to be who you really are, and then show who you really are. In doing this, you make yourself vulnerable to the possibility of an emotional wound. Many people shy away from any real connection, the very thing we want most, for exactly this reason. Why do some of us go through life avoiding the thing that will provide the most fulfillment? Fear.

I've dated men who, just before meeting me, came out of emotionally abusive long-term relationships or marriages. We had a strong connection that came naturally, but each time the connection began to deepen, they fled. What if they let themselves be vulnerable and again left the relationship emotionally or financially damaged? Keeping their distance was a way to avoid pain. But then they will always feel a little, if not a lot, empty.

When I first moved to New York, I met a woman I became friends with for a short time who had just gotten out of a twenty-year marriage. She'd gotten a job in New York and, like me, recently moved here. She told me about her divorce and said she had no interest in getting married again or even having a serious relationship. Instead, she was on a dating spree dating lots of guys for brief periods and not letting the relationships grow past the surface level.

She and I ended our friendship after a few months as our connection didn't sit right with me. While I couldn't put it into words back then, our friendship, just like her dating spree, was only surface level. Inside she was hurt, having not yet healed from the collapse of her marriage, which takes time. She was protecting herself from getting hurt again in all areas of her life, not just in dating but even in her friendships. She exuded an air of not caring about the men she dated and also of not caring about me.

Confidence in not caring what others think is a strength contingent upon one thing: are you showing others who you really are? Are you being your true self, letting others see your good and bad qualities, your desires, and also what hurts you? Are you revealing who you are regardless of the outcome? If not, there is no risk involved. You're not risking rejection when you're not being real.

Without honesty with yourself and others, without the risk that says, "This is me. This is who I am, and this is what I want. This feels bad to me, and this feels good," there can never be a real connection. Even though I was much younger and more naïve back then when I was hanging out with my new friend, I did know something didn't feel right, and it was not a friendship I could continue. She wasn't being her authentic self with me, so there was no real closeness, and surface-level connections have never interested me.

Even some parents with good intentions and decent relationships with their kids avoid getting too close for fear of getting hurt. Maybe they withhold affection, fearing they won't get it back. Maybe they limit their interactions for fear that, as a parent, they won't be enough. It takes great strength to be vulnerable, to open up and show yourself, to say, "This is me, like it or not. I hope you like it, but that's a risk I'm willing to take."

How can you relate to each other when you don't *know* each other? How can you allow yourself to be received when you don't show your real self? How can you attract genuine friendships and partnerships when you are emotionally absent? How can you gather respect from your team members when you hide your weaknesses and emotions, the things that make you human?

Without the element of risk, there can be no payoff. When you pretend to be someone you're not, if someone likes you, they're not liking the real you. On a subconscious level, this hurts less. But then, you avoid any chance of a real connection. To have true connection and acceptance, the commonality we all seek if we're being honest, you must show who you really are. In any gain, there was always a risk first.

Vulnerability in Leaders

If vulnerability is the only way to create an opportunity for human connection, it makes sense that leaders who allow themselves to be vulnerable yield more followers. Teams will perform better when they feel understood and cared about. Caring comes from understanding, first stimulated by connection, which starts with letting yourself be vulnerable.

You cannot truly be accepted by others without first letting yourself open up and be vulnerable to them. Perhaps the most effective way to flex your leadership muscles, whether you're leading a team or leading your own life, is to start by being vulnerable. Let others see you. Aren't true stories the most captivating? Let others see what you're really about. Intrigue them.

An article in Harvard Business Review, *What Bosses Gain from Being Vulnerable*, discusses why vulnerability is a strength, particularly for leaders, and how employees are more likely to make sacrifices for a leader they have a personal relationship with.[7] The article goes on to discuss how being vulnerable is part of being courageous and also mentions the theory I outlined, that connection starts with vulnerability.

Yourself Is your Calling Card

When you release the weight of trying to portray someone you're not, not only do you begin navigating life more easily, feeling lighter and freer, you also create room for and become more magnetic to the people and opportunities with whom you naturally align.

I lived the first half of my life trying to be someone I was not. I didn't realize I was doing this out of fear that others might not accept me. Instead, I thought my attempt was out of consideration for others. I didn't want to bother anyone by taking the risk of being myself. It's my nature to be direct—very direct. This is how I communicate.

For me, anything less than straight-to-the-point honesty feels unnatural. To me, it actually feels bad, really bad. Still, I understand many people are not comfortable with direct honesty. My attempts to put others' comfort ahead of my own left *me* feeling very uncomfortable for years. I felt consistently and increasingly disconnected, and I was very unhappy. In portraying someone I was not, I was attracting the wrong people. I felt empty.

---

[7] Emma Seppälä, "What Bosses Gain by Being Vulnerable," Harvard Business Review, December 11, 2014, https://hbr.org/2014/12/what-bosses-gain-by-being-vulnerable.

If you find yourself feeling disconnected, I invite you to ask yourself a question: Are you *being* yourself?

When I finally grew uncomfortable enough, I decided not only to start being myself but to be 1000% myself. Instead of trying to quiet my directness, I would be even *more* direct because that feels natural and good to me. Not only did I begin feeling better, letting go of the pressure of trying to be someone I wasn't, but I also began attracting people that liked me for exactly who I am.

I had been leading a life where, despite my persistent efforts to feel fulfilled, there was always an underlying feeling of emptiness. I carried it with me like I carried my keys. It was just there, and the reason why was I had been living my life, to some degree, trying to be someone I wasn't. I now have close friends who don't mind my directness; they even appreciate it. Some are even more direct than I, which I love.

Pay close attention to how you feel in certain company. If something doesn't feel right to you, that's an indicator pointing you in a different direction. Honor yourself by being honest. If you find that you can't be honest with those around you, you're likely not being honest with yourself. And if you're not being honest with yourself, how can you feel good?

Yourself is actually your calling card. What and who do you want to attract? When you listen to and honor your feelings, to what feels right and what doesn't, you are heading in the right direction. The more *yourself* you are as much of the time as possible, the less likely you are to feel disconnected.

The desire to feel accepted is behind what makes you sometimes try and squeeze yourself into a shape that doesn't fit.

And when you're not being authentically yourself, you're uncomfortable. Ironically, when you decide just to be 1000% yourself, turn your focus inward, and follow what feels right, you establish the only foundation from which you can truly gain acceptance.

If you realize you're perhaps not being yourself, the solution is simple. Just start. Those who like it will be attracted to you. Those who don't will continue on their way. It may take a little time to align with like-minded people and the opportunities you're seeking, but it will happen. The alternative is to keep moving in a direction with people and things that don't feel right.

So even when it may seem like the people and opportunities are taking a long time to come in, know that you're on the right track. Invest in yourself by doing things you enjoy and find fulfillment there. In fulfilling yourself, when you do align with those who are meant to walk your journey with you, you will have more to offer.

Fearlessness Is Allowing Yourself to Feel

Winston Churchill, one of the most revered leaders of all time, battled depression. Martin Luther King was not afraid to admit, "I have a dream." Mahatma Gandhi inspired millions of followers by preaching love and peace. Nelson Mandela was not afraid to admit he was deeply pained by racism.

Leaders whose names live on in the history books, as well as those who captivate, motivate, and encourage on a lesser-known scale, are not afraid to admit when something bothers them. The act of standing up and speaking out to create change is an admission of vulnerability. *This bothers me* is a degree of *this hurts me,* and *so I'm going to do something about it.* This is how leaders start. The glimmer that ignites the spark that feeds the flame is an admission of an emotion. Leaders are not afraid to feel. It makes sense, then, that your best leaders are the most relatable. They are people you can understand.

Who do you trust more—someone who is open, honest, and real? Or someone hiding their true feelings, and thus, their true self, from you? You trust people who feel. Why do you love movies and actors? You can relate to them and their vulnerability. You can't relate to a character who doesn't exude emotion. You don't trust or like them. You change the channel. You tune in when someone is authentic and tune out when they are not.

Leaders are survivors. Bottling up emotions not only eliminates the opportunity for closeness, it also increases your mortality rate. You hear of people "reaching their breaking point" or having a "mental breakdown." This sounds to me more like strength rather than weakness. This is the body's way of caring for itself. When the mind resists, attempting to ignore how it feels and what it needs, eventually, the body wins the struggle, taking what it needs. And thank goodness. The alternative could be heart disease, or diabetes. Want to be a survivor? Let people see who you are, including your emotions, the good, the bad, and the sometimes ugly.

Could it be vulnerability that propels leaders toward their achievements? While you may not have ambitions to lead a team or start a company, you do lead your own life. If you're feeling disconnected, try letting yourself be vulnerable.

Vulnerability in Men

Like many others, I grew up in a family of men who did not show their emotions, aside from my maternal grandfather, who has always been affectionate, open, and expressive. However, my father, his father, and my stepfather were not as comfortable baring their feelings. I wager they were also uncomfortable acknowledging their feelings within themselves.

Acknowledging your feelings provides an opportunity for you to experience them, and since not every emotion feels good, feeling your feelings means opening yourself up to sometimes experience pain. And showing you're in pain can leave you feeling exposed. But your emotions are there, whether you acknowledge or show them. When you show your emotions and let yourself become vulnerable, you allow the opportunity for closeness, connection, and to be understood. Doesn't that sound nice, refreshing, and comforting?

Baring the weight of unexpressed emotion eventually becomes impossible, sometimes resulting in losing your temper or, on a smaller scale, overreacting. Research shows it's also why you sometimes get sick. Over time, unexpressed feelings can weaken your immune system. According to a 2013 study by the Harvard School of Public Health and the University of Rochester, "People who bottle up their emotions increased their chance of premature death from all causes by more than 30%, with their risk of being diagnosed with cancer increasing by 70%."[8]

---

[8] Benjamin P. Chapman Chapman, Benjamin P., Kevin Fiscella, Ichiro Kawachi, Paul Duberstein, and Peter Muennig, "Emotion Suppression and Mortality Risk over a 12-Year Follow-Up," *Journal of Psychosomatic Research* 75, no. 4 (October 2013): pp. 381-385, https://doi.org/10.1016/j.jpsychores.2013.07.014.

As my fathers and grandfathers grew older, I watched them become more emotional, more expressive, and even tear up at times. Interestingly, I have never seen my maternal grandfather cry, the one who always openly expresses his emotions, probably because he doesn't have anything bottled up. My stepfather, father, and his father, on the other hand, had some emotions to release. Holding them in finally became too much.

One of my favorite things on Thanksgiving is having everyone go around the table and say one thing they are thankful for. The last time we did this at my mother's house, my stepfather broke down when it came to his turn. "I'm just thankful for … everything at this table," he said, and he started to cry. He could barely get the words out.

Leaders Take Risks

Your challenges will each be unique. Acknowledging the walls you come up against is not what makes you weak. It is, instead, the first step in learning to navigate your way through, over, or around them, which makes you strong. Getting to the other side of that wall, figuratively speaking, is success. And winning your inner battles reveals the strength you had within you all along. The wall, the challenge, is there to show you who you really are, to help you become that better version of yourself. To uncover who you really are, you must first admit there is something you struggle with.

Chapter 9 Exercise: Identify and Take a Risk

Successful people take risks. Risk implies vulnerability. Think of a risk you have taken in your life. What was the outcome? Take a moment to write it down. If there is an element of dissatisfaction anywhere in your life, then there is a risk that needs to be taken. Consider what might happen if you try being more vulnerable in that area by admitting what you want, first to yourself and then to others. Then take a bigger risk by beginning your pursuit.

Master your Mindset

1. Choose to be like the leaders you look up to: vulnerable.

2. *Yourself* is your calling card. If you're feeling disconnected, ask yourself if you are *being* yourself.

3. Take risks. Start with something small and increase your confidence as you go.

Some Extra Encouragement ...

It's okay sometimes to feel scared. It's your choices that dictate your future.

Next, we will talk more about fear and how to beat it every time. You can learn to use fear as a tool. If fear-based thoughts can keep you stuck—stuck inside of your house, stuck in your unfulfilling job, stuck in an empty relationship, or from pursuing your passion, what could positive and abundant thoughts do? In the next chapter, you will tackle fear so that when it shows up, you recognize the right path.

Chapter Ten

Beating Fear

Chapter 10: Tackling Fear

How to Never Make Another Mistake

> "The only thing we have to fear is fear itself."
> ~*FDR*

What came first? The chicken or the egg?

Somehow, I have always inherently known that there is enough success to go around for everyone. This abundant mindset lies at the root of my drive to succeed and to get up and try again. Did my lack of fear inspire my belief in myself? Or did my belief in myself secure the awareness that I would always have more than I need?

It's ironic that a woman fearless in pursuing whatever she sets her mind to, was once riddled with fear so debilitating she was afraid to leave her house. But we are all on different paths learning different lessons, and the more you *over*come, the more you *be*come.

Abundant: *plentiful; more than enough.*

Would you agree that the most successful people have abundance? In order to have abundance, you must first believe it's possible. If one believes they can have more than enough, wouldn't they also believe others can too?

An abundant mindset is the opposite of fear-based. If an abundant mindset, as you just considered, leads to a full life, then couldn't a fear-based mindset easily lead to a life of lack? Couldn't fear even then be the reason for whatever's not working in your life?

If there's something you'd like to change, are you curious and brave enough to change it? You can remain on the figurative starting block – the one you will still be standing on—this time next year, or you can choose to shift your mindset. While you can't yet see past your first step, if you take a step, you're moving. When you reach the end of the first block, you will see the next. But you must be moving. You have to take that first step. If you want something new and different, your direction must be new and different.

What if I told you that any direction is the right direction? Just move. Once you're moving, you will get bumped on the right path for you. But you do have to first listen to what you want, tell yourself you can, and then start. Once you start, aren't you further down your path?

Another wise woman once said, "In your true place, there is no competition." This means that when you are doing what is meant for you, you will be great at it. Maybe someone else will also be great, in a way that is uniquely their own. Can you imagine if, after the first great love story, all the other screenwriters in this genre put down their pens? You would be missing out on some inspirational and heart-warming stories. While there are probably thousands of influencers and motivational speakers, certain messages resonate with certain people, and the people who need the messages meant for them will align. Someone is seeking what you have to offer. When you keep yourself from offering it, you deny the world your gifts.

Feeling Indecisive? Get Primal

Before logic kicks in, your instincts are always at work, attempting to sway your direction in just one way.

Logic can help to the same degree it can hinder, but only after you follow your instincts. Your instincts always lead you in only one direction—forward or back, toward or away. It's when you ignore or try to quiet your instincts that you get yourself into trouble. How do you break this bad habit? Let's start with something your logical mind looks for: proof.

Have you ever watched a movie and could tell who the bad guy was before anything even happened? Have you ever had a conversation and knew there was something the other person wasn't saying? Have you ever gone on a job interview and known it wasn't for you? But you went on a second interview, and then a third, only to feel increasingly uncomfortable? Have you ever dated someone you felt was lying to you? Did you ignore your instincts and go on a second date and a third, and before you knew it, you were six months or a year into a bad relationship that was becoming increasingly painful?

Looking back, you can easily see what would have been a better path. You also likely remember the exact moment your intuition kicked in, trying to guide and protect you. Why didn't you listen? Fear. Fear that something or someone better for you might not show up. You created the miserable place, job, or relationship you later found yourself in by choosing to let your fear, rather than your intuition, guide you.

If you recognize you've made this mistake, be easy on yourself. I've done it before, too, many times. That's the only reason I'm qualified to talk about it. I'll share another comforting concept. When you ignore your intuition, it doesn't mean you won't find your way. The way is still there; it might just take you longer to find. Why not speed up the process and get where you want faster by succumbing to your intuition?

Fear vs. Intuition

When you get an idea for something, this is your instinct guiding you. It may take some planning and sacrifice to ultimately achieve your goal, but your instincts are leading you in the right direction to help get you started. Once you get going, you can then employ logic to carry you further. But your instincts will be showing you the way. Let your intuition be your torch, and let your logic follow.

Your instincts never fail you. They are as reliable as the sun coming up. When they fail at keeping you safe, it's because you didn't listen.

It's ironic that someone so good at listening to her instincts for career and life direction, adamantly ignored the blazing red flags in her dating life. As I said, we all have different walls to learn how to navigate our way through or around. But when you do, the ultimate reward shows up for you on the other side—happiness.

Following my instincts in life and career has led me further and made me happier, while ignoring my instincts in relationships kept me stuck in the very same place for most of my adult life—hurt and wondering what went wrong. Looking back with my new perspective, it's easy to see what went wrong. I ignored my instincts.

Red Flags

Walking in Manhattan, with so many people in such close proximity, I often catch snippets of other people's conversations. It can be quite comical hearing phrases out of context. One cloudy evening on my way to yoga, I overheard this guy's conversation. He was venting to an apparent stranger while walking his dog.

"She kept almost hitting my dog in the face with her umbrella! After saying 'Excuse me,' multiple times, I finally said, '*Look lady, you're about to hit my dog in the face with your umbrella,*'" he told the guy, who listened as they walked. His story amused me, and I was walking in the same direction, so I kept listening. *"'You need to watch where you're going,'* she said. So I told her, her husband needs to keep her in line; *'oh wait, you probably don't have one.' 'You look like you're alone too,'* she said."

I laughed out loud.

"Anyway, thanks for letting me vent, man. *Have a nice day."* The man turned at the corner and, feeling playful, I chimed in. "You're welcome," I said.

He turned around. "Oh, you were listening too?"

This was the start of a miserable relationship that I would later learn should have ended at the next block. We were instantly attracted to each other, and I let my attraction (and my fear) override the fact that this guy was already getting on my last nerve within two blocks of meeting him. He asked me questions to try and get to know me, and each time I started to answer, he would interrupt and again start talking about himself. The one-sided conversation he'd had with the stranger a moment before was how he had all of his conversations.

I ignored my intuition and gave him my number. I ignored it again, later keeping our first date when he was an hour late, and still, I ignored it again when he constantly interrupted me on the date. I continued to ignore all the red flags that flared giant warning signals around 90 percent of my experiences with him.

Six months later, and feeling more miserable and frustrated than ever, I finally had no choice but to never see him again. I could have avoided all of the unnecessary pain brought on by this completely dysfunctional relationship with a completely dysfunctional guy had I listened to my very first gut instinct, which came within about ten seconds of meeting him.

The Universe Has Your Back

When you ignore your instincts, your problems get bigger until you are forced to start paying attention. And when you still don't get yourself on the right path, the Universe steps in.

One evening, after wrapping up an open mic, back in the days when I stayed up late, I was excited to head to my favorite night spot for some music and dancing. My plans were in place, and I was sure to enjoy myself. Then something happened. A guy reached out and wanted to get together. I knew him enough to know that I would likely enjoy his company and told him my plans and that he could come along if he liked.

He suggested another place to meet. This was my first mistake. I ignored my instincts to stick with my plans and agreed to meet where he suggested. On my way, the Universe tried to intervene. I was en route on the subway and listening to my headphones; I didn't hear the announcement over the loudspeaker that the subway was being rerouted and would be going way past my stop. Minutes later, I looked up, confused and now inconvenienced, and very far away from where I was trying to go. The Universe was diverting me. Things weren't working out, and I later learned that was for a good reason.

The Night My Instincts Kept Me ... Clean

I was heading home one evening and walking down the sidewalk, I suddenly heard this voice inside my head telling me to cross the street. I did eventually need to cross the street, as I lived on the other side. But I wasn't even to the next intersection, and I still had a block and a half to go before reaching my building.

I ignored the voice and kept walking. The voice persisted, growing louder. I kept ignoring it. It persisted. "Cross the street immediately! Do it right now!" I was literally having this silent, yet very loud, conversation in my head. Finally, I gave in, "Okay already, I'll cross the street." While I felt no apparent danger, the second I stepped off the sidewalk and into the street, a guy appeared. I had not seen him the moment before. He was tall and skinny, and you'll never guess what he did. He threw up all over the sidewalk, exactly where I would have been standing.

Life is a ride, no matter your choices—the key to what kind of ride is the choices you make. When you go against your intuition, you naturally make the ride bumpier than necessary. But how do you know for sure whether it's fear or your intuition talking?

As always, the answer is in your emotions. How do you feel when you first get an idea for something new you want to try, improve or change? Excited? Curious? Observe what happens next and pay attention to the timeline of your thoughts. What thought came after the emotion of excitement?

"What if I can't?"

"What if it doesn't work out?"

How do you feel when focusing on these thoughts? Discouraged? A drop in energy? If you peel back the layers, you feel scared. This is okay. It's okay to be scared. It's what you do next that determines your path. Many of us let fear stop us from ever getting started.

If you want to keep living the exact life you're living, make the same choices you made yesterday. But before you decide, let's go back to becoming an observer. Take a moment, take a breath, and take a step outside of yourself. As an objective observer, can you open your mind to the possibility that the new excitement-generating thought or idea came to you for a reason? Can you let yourself wonder if maybe there is something different meant for you?

Go back to the emotion that came right after the thought. Excitement. Remind yourself that your choices create your life. You have the power to make your own choices, which means you have the power to make different choices. If the choices you make create your life, and you make your own choices, don't you, in essence, create your life? If you create your life, doesn't that mean you have the power to create the life you want?

When in doubt, remember that anytime a decision is based on fear, it's the wrong decision; unless of course, you're in physical danger. If you choose the choice that scares you, you will most certainly create a new outcome. When you do, not only do you quickly move in the right direction, you change. You just beat fear, because once you choose the scary choice, you're no longer scared, until you come up against the next thing.

But now you're stronger. You've beat fear once by listening to your instincts, either following the positive emotion toward a better direction, or by heeding a warning and keeping yourself emotionally safe. Either way, you're happier and further along your path. You proved that you can trust your instincts. Once you do something for the first time, not only can you do it again, but it becomes easier. Simply repeat the process.

You are the creator. When you understand this, life gets easier and more fulfilling; you can achieve the things you want, living the life you want, and also catapult yourself to where you want to be. You become a mega manifester. Want to live an easy, happy life? Become fearless by doing what scares you.

This is how you beat fear so that eventually, it never shows up again. When you do something for the very first time, you're in unfamiliar territory. You're scared. You haven't done it before, so you haven't yet seen the outcome. Once you do it just once, the next time it's more comfortable.

I found myself a little nervous for the first boxing class I went to in the city. I was in a new place with people I didn't know who all knew each other. I could have stuck with what I knew, running and yoga. But I had felt drawn to the class for a reason. I wanted to try something different. I loved it; it was an incredible workout. The next time I went, I was less nervous. I knew what to expect, and I knew I was going to feel amazing after.

Truthfully, I was always just a little nervous in that class as I had a crush on the instructor. But I went with my first instinct, which was to try the class. I pushed fear aside and tried something out of my element.

I had many great workouts, and I also had a new experience with the cute instructor I had felt so drawn to. He ended up being a catalyst for yet another emotional growth spurt. My relationship with him was one of my more painful dating experiences. But it stimulated the exploration and, finally, the excavation of the root issue from which my lifetime of unhappiness stemmed. Through my experiences with him, I was forced to dig deeper to uncover the truth of what had been holding me back in certain areas of my life. Not only did I find the answers, I found what I had been searching for, and I was able to give myself exactly what that was.

The Universe has plans for you, and sometimes you have to go through a lot of pain to get where you're meant to be. But when you follow your instincts and let them guide you, you do get there.

How to Navigate Life

In Chapter One, we talked about how overcoming is becoming. Once you overcome, looking back, no matter how painful the experience, you don't seem to have regrets because you learned something invaluable. While life's lessons can often be painful, they don't have to be. The more you learn to trust your intuition and heed your instincts, the less pain you encounter.

Sometimes you meet resistance that doesn't feel like a positive challenge, but instead just hurts. Sometimes you find yourself frustrated in a stagnant situation. When this happens, rather than stubbornly try to push past a wall that won't budge, consider that something is telling you to go a different way. Be easy on yourself and explore a new path, one that will be better for you. Sometimes it's best to let go, allow, surrender, and let life bump you in a less frustrating direction.

Remember to Get Excited

Successful people envision their goals and dreams with such certainty as if they are already accomplished. How else could they have achieved them? What makes them different? Their thoughts. If your thoughts are leading you in a direction you don't like, change them.

Make a daily practice of conjuring up the emotion of excitement around your ambitions and genuine gratitude as you picture yourself achieving. You will find that starting each day with these emotions will lead to new ideas, which will lead to new choices and the new life you create for yourself.

Having ups and downs will still happen, but you will learn how to quickly pick yourself up when you feel a little down. And the downs will never be as low as they once might have been. Once you elevate yourself to new levels, you are elevated.

Chapter 10 Exercise: Identify Fear and Intuition

Before you turn the page, let's test your ability to distinguish fear from intuition. Look back at a past experience that did not turn out so well in the end. Try and remember back to the beginning. Was there a moment where you felt warned to go in a different direction?

Brainstorm a couple more experiences like this and write down the specific red flags you ignored. You are learning to identify *your intuition*. Moving forward, remember this exercise and those red flags so you can identify them faster and not make the same mistakes.

Master your Mindset

1. Remember, life gets easier when you follow your intuition.

2. Distinguish fear from intuition. Identify the emotion that first surfaced when considering a new idea or direction. The first emotion dictates your direction – toward or away.

Some Extra Encouragement ...

We've all had experiences in which we've ignored the red flags. Tell yourself, "Good job," for increasing your self-awareness. Be easy on yourself and do better next time. There will be a next time. With your increased self-confidence and trust in your intuition, you will make the right choice.

Still with me? Great job. You're about to start the first page of the final chapter, where you will gently lock it all in, review, and solidify what you've learned, leaving you more aware of yourself and how to best navigate your life—your *happy and abundant life*. But first, a little disclaimer:

I might get a little *"woo-woo"* on you. Not too much, but a little. I will also share the answer to your burning question. Get excited to turn the page to the final chapter. Then, get excited to turn the unexplored page of each moment of the rest of your life.

Chapter Eleven
The Deep Stuff

Chapter 11: The Deep Stuff

The Best Things Happen When You Have No Idea What's Next

> "If you can think it, you can do it."
> ~Dionne Warwick

I remember sitting quietly, buckled into the backseat of my mother's maroon Monte Carlo. My stepdad was driving, my mother was in the passenger seat, and my little brother and older sister were in the backseat alongside me. I would rest my elbow on the door with my chin in my hand, staring out the window. "Stop leaning on the door!" my stepdad's voice would bellow from the front seat.

I would roll my eyes as exaggeratedly as possible so he could see my defiance in the rearview mirror as I begrudgingly withdrew my elbow from the door. I'm not entirely sure what the harm was in my sitting like that, although I've come to understand my stepfather better more recently.

He became my stepdad when I was two years old, and he passed away just last year, as I write this in April of 2022. While he was often stern, and I felt he was mean, even into my later years, I always felt a warmth about him and for him. I wanted to be closer to him. Now that he has passed, he sometimes shows up to give me what he wasn't capable of giving when he was alive.

The *"woo-woo"* is starting earlier in the chapter than I'd originally planned. I know he's around because I feel his presence in my heart. Suddenly he will cross my mind, and then, out of nowhere, I will feel overcome with emotion while comforted at the same time. In my mind, I will hear him telling me he is proud of me, and I'll start to cry, and I'll just let myself be in that moment with him. I know he is telling me he's sorry, and I tell him it's okay, that I love him and understand.

I always wanted to know more about my stepdad growing up. I wanted to sit in his lap, talk to him, and have him tell me about his life, his childhood, and where he went to school. I remember one night I had gone to bed. I was scared of the dark and always slept with my door open. I lay awake under the covers. My stepdad climbed the stairs and started to turn down the hallway to his and my mother's room. I called out to him. "Gary?" I said. "Where did you go to school?"

"I went to a trade school," he said. And he kept walking.

After he passed, I learned more about how difficult his life was growing up. He didn't have his father in his life. He did have a stepfather, who was abusive, and my stepfather stepped up and stood up for his mother at just 14 years old. He began working to take care of his mother and two younger sisters. While my stepdad had a good relationship with his son, my younger brother, I learned that he didn't open up to him either. My mother told me about times when she felt frustrated with him for not taking the lead in certain activities with my brother. And I learned he kept a distance as a means of protecting himself.

My stepdad didn't have a father to show him how to be a father, and he also didn't have a childhood to learn how to be a kid. Likely, for these reasons, it was difficult for him to be a father and to let us kids be kids, especially me. Growing up, it felt like it was only me he was hard on. He wasn't hard on my brother or nearly as hard on my older sister. But he was very hard on me, often yelling at me, grounding me, rolling his eyes disapprovingly at me. It hurt a lot, and I never really felt comfortable at home. This was the start of experiences leading to the teachings I share in this book. I'm grateful for all of my experiences. They pushed me to *become*. And I know my stepdad loves me and is proud of me.

I even believe I know why he was the hardest on me. I pushed him. I pushed him, not just in the way that kids push to assert themselves. I pushed him to do and to be things he was uncomfortable doing and being. I wanted closeness with him. He wasn't capable of that. I pushed the limits, standing up to him and my mother when I felt I was being mistreated. I talked back. I told him he was mean. I would say, *"This isn't right."* But I think, mostly, I made him feel uncomfortable because I wanted closeness with him, and I pushed for it.

There I was, someone in his own home, someone he kept safe and provided for, and I was making him uncomfortable. What could he do? What do you do when you're uncomfortable with something? Unless you are open and ready to work on yourself, you try to ignore the problem. You dismiss it; you pretend it's not there. While he made sure I had what I needed, he also tried to make me go away in his own way, finding reasons to ground me to the confines of my room for weeks at a time. I spent half of the time restricted to my room from the age of 11 to 15 until finally, I moved to Kansas to live with my dad.

My brother and sister were free to play with friends and come and go, seemingly as they pleased. Not me. I was trapped in my room, feeling sorry for myself. My brother and sister didn't push. My brother had no need to as he was allowed to do whatever he wanted, and my sister just has a very different personality than I. She's more of a pacificist who said herself—she "tries to keep the peace." I'm the opposite. I have no problem confronting the issue because I know that's the only way to resolve it. And I also inherently know that it is my job to solve problems and help others learn about themselves by being honest.

Yes, it's scary. Yes, it's hard. Yes, it pushes the people who should be closest to me the furthest from me, and this has been a big part of what was once a pain-filled life for me. But where is the peace when you cannot be honest with yourself and others for fear that they will leave or not accept you?

When there is an unpleasant emotion or a significant disagreement, the only way around the problem is to address the exact problem. Talk about it. It's okay to come away still in disagreement. Is it not okay to have an opinion? A point of view? Of course, it is. But there is no peace when you cannot share yours with the people closest to you. I stood up, and I fought back. But I was the only one in the house who did this, deeming me *a problem* in the eyes of my family.

So I think I understand why my stepdad was mean to me growing up and, likely, why he didn't want me resting my little chin in my little hand in the backseat of the car. I was trying to be me. I was trying to express myself. And self-expression is something he was uncomfortable with. The "me" that I truly was, I think made him feel uncomfortable. "It's okay, Dad."

Your pain is often, or always, your catalyst driving your pull, what it is you feel called to do in the unique way that only you can. The painful events or challenges you overcome equip you to become your greatest potential.

Back to Dreaming

Sitting in the back of the maroon Monte Carlo, unhappily resting my hands in my lap, I would stare out the window, looking at the trees, my little mind wandering. I would think up stories in my head. One would lead to the next, leading to the next, until, far away in dreamland, I'd open my mouth after a long period of silence to ask my mother a question. She would say, "How did you think of that?"

My mind still wanders like this. It is always exploring—myself, others, and new dreams and ideas. Isn't this how kids approach the world? I think they have it right—kids dream. Kids get excited, jumping out of bed early in the morning to begin their day, sneaking into the kitchen while everyone else is asleep, taking great joy in pouring their bowl of cereal, then into the living room to play with their toys or watch their favorite show. They're excited to wake up, to move, to explore.

Kids don't say, *"What if I fall down again?"* Kids just get up.

Kids express their emotions. They cry when they're sad, scream when angry, and hug when they feel love. Kids may not be aware of their ability to express their feelings, but they do express them. This keeps them emotionally healthy while allowing closeness with others.

Kids allow themselves to be vulnerable. They haven't yet learned to hold their cards, to portray strength when they might feel scared. This ability to be vulnerable provides a landscape for them to give and receive love. Without letting others see you, there is no true connection. True connection comes from within, and you limit yourself when all you show is your surface. Living your fullest life means not only exploring and offering your gifts; it also means connecting with the people you feel drawn to, learning and growing from each other.

Kids stay curious. They ask "*why*," unafraid to dig for and find the answers. Kids have not yet discovered their ego. When you are in your ego, you are in a primitive state of defense. If you peel back a layer, ego is fear-based. When you are in this state, you are making self-serving choices that keep you separate and disconnected.

If the natural state is a connection to your community, then when you keep yourself separate, you will certainly feel disharmony. In this state, you base your decisions on fear—fear that you won't be accepted if you show your true self. When you're not showing your true self, how can you attract those with whom you resonate or want to resonate with? Instead, you will attract others who are vibrating in your primitive, fear-based energy. Guarding yourself in defense makes for tumultuous and painful relationships, and I know from plenty of experience.

Remember to Be Easy on Yourself

If you're feeling overwhelmed by the responsibility of the inner work you may have discovered is needed, take a deep breath, and relax into your exhale. Remember to be easy on yourself. Take some pressure off by reminding yourself that you were born knowing how to do everything you've covered so far in this book. You were once a kid—vulnerable, expressive, excited, and filled with wonder.

Where to start? Start by getting curious. What you choose to get curious about depends on how you're feeling. Let's take a step back before you get curious and instead start with observing your emotions. Sit and take notice of how you're feeling. Is something bugging you? Remember, discomfort is a great thing because it means you're ready for change. Approaching discomfort with the attitude of acceptance, curiosity, and then excitement, is comforting.

Sit with the uncomfortable emotion; observe it. Let it come up. *Feel* rather than avoid it. Take the pressure to feel better out of the equation, and just let yourself feel how you're feeling. There is surprising comfort in doing this. It's a way of caring for yourself, babying yourself. Much like when you're sick, and you comfort yourself with soup, a blanket, and good sleep, you can comfort yourself when you don't feel good in your emotions by letting yourself feel how you feel. Then go deeper by asking yourself some questions:

Why are you feeling the way you're feeling?

What is it that's really bugging you about what's bugging you?

This step is important because it stimulates action. Different actions create different outcomes—no pressure to move into action just yet. After you acknowledge your emotions and get curious about them, you will likely uncover the deeper issue that is actually bothering you. Once you know what it is, tell yourself, "Good job," and relax. Don't focus on it anymore for the moment. Remember, you become equipped to solve the real problem once you identify it. Get present and get excited for the change that is coming. Get involved in an activity you feel like doing or need to get done. Get to work, tackle your to-do list, or get in a workout. You will feel better refocusing your thoughts.

Next, pay attention. Continue working to stay present during your daily activities. If you're with someone, give them 100% of your focus when they're talking. If you're walking around, observe your surroundings. Really look at the people, the trees, the buildings. By staying present, you will be open and receiving of opportunities you might otherwise miss.

Take notice when you get an idea. You've observed how you're feeling, letting the emotion surface. You focused on it, went deeper, and uncovered the real issue that was truly bothering you. You got present, going about your day. When you get an idea, which you will, this is the answer to your problem coming right to you. You won't have to look for it; it will just show up. You'll know it's the solution to your problem, again, by observing your emotions. What emotion directly follows your new idea right when you think of it? Excitement? Bingo. You have found your new direction.

What happens next? The need to know *how* comes in. With your new present, curious and excitable mindset, it's your job to ward off *the how*:

But how is this going to happen?

What if it doesn't work?

This is human nature. You are working to change your mindset. *"What if I can't?"* becomes *"What if I can? What if it does work?" "Of course I can." "Yes, it will."* All you have to do is begin to observe how you're thinking. The moment you choose to observe you're your thoughts, actions and reactions, is the moment you create change.

In staying present, you will get another idea, which will be your first step onto your new path leading in your new direction. You will know it's the right move, again, by your emotions around it. Do you feel excited? Good job. It's Go Time.

Many of us get stopped at *the how*. You want to know what the tenth step looks like before you take the first. There is no actual way to know what's coming. You cannot know who you will meet to help you on your way. You can't know the exact job you will move into, the exact child you will have, or how you will meet your next love. But by getting excited about and even grateful for your future, having faith and trust in the Universe, in your intuition, and your ability to create, the steps do show up, one after the next.

If you need a little encouragement, maybe some proof that your new choices will create your new future, let's consider when you decide to go out to dinner. When you go to the same place you usually go with the same friend you usually go with, sitting in the same seat you normally sit in, and ordering the same dish you typically order, you will have one experience. You will have a completely different experience when you choose a different spot. Not to say that one will be better than the other in this scenario, but different choices bring different outcomes. If you'd like a different outcome, try a different choice.

The greatest kind of empowerment is self-empowerment. The answers are, and always were, within you. Once you awaken this superpower, you never need to look outside yourself for the answers.

Life is a practice of continuous self-improvement once you begin the journey. You will notice that the more you practice self-awareness, observing your emotions, actions, and state of mind, the better the journey gets. And with each level you raise your vibration, the downs become higher and less frequent. When you make positive choices for yourself, your overall state of mind elevates and does not descend. When you have a dip, you also know how to pick yourself back up quickly.

While it's necessary to focus on your emotions to ultimately identify and overcome what's holding you back, it is also important to feel good as much of the time as possible. When you feel a little down, acknowledge it, then do something to get feeling good again. You attract more of how you're feeling. At the end of this chapter, I'll include some pick-me-up resources to help get and keep yourself feeling good.

Releasing Anger

Letting go of past hurts can be challenging. But it actually does not have to be nearly as hard as you make it on yourself. At times we don't understand how someone could treat us the way they did. Remember, you project onto others how you are feeling about yourself. When you're not in a great mood, you're not your best to others. When something is bothering you, you often project, taking it out on those around you. And the more pain you're in, the more severe your reactions. The same is true for others and their actions toward us.

When you're more advanced in self-awareness, self-management, and actively practicing observing your emotions so they don't control you, you get better at choosing different reactions and releasing anger. And when you learn to give yourself what you need, you no longer need it from the past people who hurt you or from anyone else. Then the anger just goes away by itself. This is not to say that you accept ill-treatment from others. Instead, you give yourself the kindness you need by being discerning. You further empower yourself to choose who and what you give your time and energy to.

Through this process of releasing anger, the pain will sometimes show up again. There have been several times when I'm moving along happily through my day feeling good, and, all of a sudden, I find myself feeling upset over something from the past. Each time I think, *"Why is this showing up?"*

When this happens, you just quickly take yourself through the process again. Just as you would comfort a small child, you can comfort yourself in much the same way. Acknowledge your feelings and remind yourself that how you feel is okay. Give yourself what you need. Maybe it's alone time or a nice long walk or run. Then also *tell* yourself what you need to hear. Maybe you want to hear from someone else that you are loved. You are special. You are talented. You are interesting. You are desirable. You have special gifts that only you can give in the way that only you can. Take a moment right now to go ahead and read back aloud those words. Tell yourself out loud that you are these things, or whichever things you would like to hear. Go ahead. I'll do it with you.

Healing Untrue Belief Systems

While kids have the right idea in many ways, they don't yet know how to care for themselves. As an experienced and capable adult, you do. You can care for yourself by giving yourself what you need. When kids go through a deeply painful experience without yet having the tools to cope, they must do something. What you did as a child is form untrue belief systems—untrue beliefs about yourself.

If, for example, a child is not receiving the love they need from a parent, maybe the belief they form about themselves is that they are unlovable. Maybe the action they then choose to cope is to chase love. The action becomes a pattern; its roots buried deep within. The problem wants to be solved, and surface-level challenges serving as triggers will keep coming up invoking the same emotion. If you felt unloved and unvalued as a child, you will feel this same emotion when relationships don't work out, or when a coworker you're trying to connect with ignores you. You feel triggered, not understanding why because the real reason, the real problem, is buried deep.

The problems you face in your life do not necessarily have to mean that you had bad parents. Everyone's experience will be different. Children are very impressionable, and even something seemingly small and unintentional can not only deeply hurt their feelings but also impact how they feel about and see themselves from that moment forward until they go back and undo the untrue belief they then formed about themselves as a result.

Chapter 11: The Deep Stuff

You can undo these untrue belief systems you formed about yourself. When you feel triggered, observe how you're feeling. What is the emotion? Then peel back some layers to uncover the deeper, underlying *untrue* emotion. For example, if you are feeling sad, *why* are you feeling sad? Keep digging deeper with a series of *why* questions until you get to the root issue. Once you uncover what it is, tell yourself the opposite:

I am lovable.

I am worthy of making money.

I am great just as I am.

I am smart.

In the way that you want someone else to accept you for you, you can learn to accept yourself. That's the real issue. When you give yourself what you need, you no longer need it from any source outside yourself. Then you become what you are capable of—a force, a power, a love-filled being that makes choices to care for yourself and, ultimately, to attract what you *are*: abundance.

The answers are always much closer than you think. What you may have been searching for your entire life, you come to learn, was inside you all along.

"That which you most want to find will be found where you least want to look."

~*Carl Jung*

When you are able to have compassion for yourself, you can more easily extend compassion to others who may not be treating you well, even if from a necessary distance. You attract more of how you feel. If something is bothering you, it needs your attention. Get curious about what's bothering you, even when it hurts to focus on it. It will hurt. But when you ignore your problems, they just keep following you around, growing bigger, which hurts too.

Remember to be easy on yourself as you step out onto your path—the path to feeling better and healing deep-seated issues or embarking on the pursuit of your new goal. It will be hard. And that is okay. A shift in perspective, as simple as telling yourself you can, even when you might not believe it just yet, makes the difference. And don't worry about how. Just get curious and start; the first step will show up and then the next. Each day will get easier. My journey to feeling better lasted decades. But yours doesn't have to.

What's Condiments Got to Do With It?

"Get the mustard!" my sister-in-law called out from the kitchen. I was visiting my brother and his family, and one of them had burnt themselves while cooking. "Why mustard?" I said. My sister-in-law shared that she once burnt her arm on the stove while visiting my parents and cooking dinner for them. My stepdad pulled the mustard out of the fridge and put it on her arm, telling her it was a natural remedy to heal faster and prevent scarring.

"Oh," I said, looking down at the inch-long scar on my forearm from the time I had burnt *my* arm in my parents' kitchen.

Where was my fucking mustard? I thought to myself.

People do what they know how. We are all on our own journeys walking around with different past experiences.

Chapter 11: The Deep Stuff

Sometimes what others do is great, and sometimes it's not so great. I found the figurative mustard I was searching for once I learned to give myself my own mustard. Then I began to feel whole. I no longer needed to look outside myself for the love, comfort, and acceptance I had been searching for my whole life. The secret is, I had it all along, and much closer than I realized. But often, you have to dig to discover the answers.

Overcoming and becoming through your painful catalysts will likely be the most challenging voyage of your lifetime. It's worth the excavation.

Thanks for coming on the journey with me, the journey that has now equipped me to help others overcome and become faster. I hope what you've learned from our time together propels you on your quest forward. I believe in You.

Much love,

~Amy

Resources to Explore:

I highly recommend seeking out content from these additional authors, speakers, and professionals whose insights have been instrumental in my growth. Judging by their following, they have helped countless others as well. Become a seeker by beginning to research what interests you and what you're curious about. When you find someone or something that speaks to you, keep going. Read more books, listen to more videos, and research new interests as they come. You will end up stumbling upon answers you never knew you were searching for.

~*Amy*

Eckhart Tolle

Don Miguel Ruiz

Deepak Chopra

Dr. Joe Dispenza

Dr. Jordan Peterson

Dr. Jeffrey Schwartz

Emotional Intelligence 2.0 by Travis Bradberry and Jean Greaves

Soul Contracts by Danielle MacKinnon

Eat Right for Your Type by Dr. Peter J. D'Adamo

The F-Factor Diet by Tanya Zuckerbrot, M.S., R.D.

Master Sri Akarshana

Jillz Guerin (for the ladies!)

I Love Honesty

Thank you for reading *Where's My Mustard?* Your feedback matters to me. Please take a moment to head over to Amazon and share your thoughts in an honest review. I appreciate you.

Let's connect!

I invite you to join my subscriber list to stay connected and to receive updates on future books and online offerings. I'm also available for *Success and Leadership* one-on-one and group coaching. If you would like to connect with me on a complimentary 30-minute coaching call, subscribe today to schedule your call. Here's to your success and greater happiness!

Subscribe today!
https://coaching.beingamyleemiller.com/

Email:
amy@beingamyleemiller.com

Website:
https://beingamyleemiller.com/

YouTube:
https://www.youtube.com/channel/UCj51BcYhSfEgBPHA1Uzlj2g

Instagram:
https://www.instagram.com/amyleemillercoaching

TikTok:
https://www.tiktok.com/@beingamyleemiller?lang=en

~Amy

Acknowledgments

Thank you to my good friends John Johansen, John Mabry, Eric Lubitz and Andy Pitz. Your positive energy, encouragement, and support contribute to my creativity.

Thank you to Cassandra Blackwell, Holly Corey, Trang Bui, Kathleen Brett, Esmira Kurjakovic, Catherine McGann, and Serena Di Liberto—beautiful, strong, and intelligent women whose bold, bright, and feminine energies help keep me balanced.

Thank you to Dr. Jordan Peterson and Dr. Joe Dispenza. Your wisdom and teachings have greatly impacted me and helped me continue lifting myself to new levels.

Thank you to Jeannie Culbertson. I so appreciate your genuine nature, amazing work ethic, and our connection.

Thank you to Edie Whiting for your warmth and our good times. Thank you to E.R. for all I've learned from you and for your help with the title.

Thank you, Sammy Musovic, for a place to clear my head.

Thank you to Gary Wheeler—for showing up for me.

Thank you to Alan Weiss, my grandfather. We have always had a special connection. He's one of few who really get me.

And thank you to my father, David Lee Miller, for showing me the stars, for being my biggest fan and always accepting me for me.

As I continue evolving and some energies unalign, it's good to remind myself of the many special people I do have in my life.

About the Author

Amy Lee Miller is an entrepreneur, author, and *Success and Leadership* coach. She is passionate about self-development and helping others empower themselves.

While Amy has been writing all her life, *Ready Set Recruit—The Hiring Manager's Guide to Recruiting with Confidence* was her first book, published in 2021, and inspired by her recruiting experience. She looks forward to publishing additional reference and motivational self-development books.

When not working or writing, you can find Amy running in Central Park or striking a pose in hot yoga. In her downtime, she enjoys stimulating conversation, being active, and snuggling with her adoring cat, Gilligan.

While Amy is fearless in pursuing her goals, you won't catch her ice skating or riding a bike. She likes her feet planted firmly on the ground while keeping her head in the clouds. She lives in Manhattan.

Subscribe with the link below to connect and stay updated on her future books.

coaching.beingamyleemiller.com

www.ingramcontent.com/pod-product-compliance
Lightning Source LLC
Chambersburg PA
CBHW020332010526
44119CB00002B/38